Pra

"Funny, honest, and vulnerable, this book is everything I've loved about reading Sammy Rhodes online for years. There's always a tension between the beautiful and the broken and Sammy does a masterly job of explaining and exploring that mystery."

Jon Acuff
New York Times bestselling author
of *Finish: Give Yourself the Gift of Done*

"Sammy Rhodes has a very unique talent of expressing God's love and truth in a way that is so honest and refreshingly authentic. In *Broken and Beloved*, Sammy shares stories of his own shortcomings and mistakes he made in his younger years (most of which are hilarious and cringe-worthy), and he so eloquently walks us through Jesus's life and ministry, which reaffirms the very comforting promise that we are all beloved by our God no matter how broken we may be. 'He is God's Beloved Son, yet at the cross He is broken for our sin. He bears two names on our behalf: Broken and Beloved.'"

Sean Lowe
Reality TV personality
Author of *For the Right Reasons: America's Favorite Bachelor on Faith, Love, Marriage, and Why Nice Guys Finish First*

"I once read that Fred Craddock insisted that if preachers reminded listeners of things forgotten, made them to know that God's grace was available, didn't feel put down or beat up, then they would walk away and say, 'That preacher knows us well.' Surely, if only through the written word, Sammy Rhodes is God's preacher and all who read this book will be sure they are known. With profundity and candor, comedy and tragedy, brilliance and beauty, he invites again to know that we are broken but we are beloved. If there is a word for us today, it is this one. This is a gem of a book that will be sure to encourage any reader. If you are looking for love and longing for hope, pick up and read. Joy awaits you!"

Danté Stewart
Writer, speaker
Author of *Prophesy Hope!: An Advent Reflection on Hope, Peace, Love, and Freedom*

"I am so thankful for Sammy Rhodes. The chapters in this book stand alone as rich meditations on the human experience in light of the Christian faith. But taken together, they give a helpful, compelling, and often hilarious picture of what it means for broken people to know and rest in the love of Christ. Especially perfect for those exploring questions about God and what it means to be human."

Russ Ramsey
Pastor of Christ Presbyterian Church, Cool Springs, Tennessee
Author of *The Advent of the Lamb of God*

"Few things connect with me as a reader (or a person) like humor and humble honesty, and both of those mark this book. Sammy Rhodes willingly wades in the dark waters of depression and his own failures, but not in a faux-authentic, word-vomit way. Rather, Rhodes points clearly and comfortingly to the presence and love of Jesus for broken sinners. This book is a pleasure to read and would be an encouraging challenge to people at any point in their faith."

Barnabas Piper
Podcaster and author of *The Pastor's Kid: Finding Your Own Faith and Identity* and *Help My Unbelief: Why Doubt Is Not the Enemy of Faith*

Broken *and* Beloved

Broken
and
Beloved

HOW JESUS LOVES US INTO WHOLENESS

Sammy Rhodes

SALEM
BOOKS

an imprint of Regnery Publishing

Scriptures marked ESV are taken from THE HOLY BIBLE, ENGLISH STANDARD VERSION® Copyright© 2001 by Crossway, a publishing ministry of Good News Publishers. Used by permission.

Scriptures marked NIV are taken from THE HOLY BIBLE, NEW INTERNA-TIONAL VERSION® Copyright© 1973, 1978, 1984, 2011 by Biblica, Inc.™ Used by permission of Zondervan.

Salem Books™ is a trademark of Salem Communications Holding Corporation
Regnery® is a registered trademark of Salem Communications Holding Corporation

ISBN: 978-1-68451-002-3
eISBN: 978-1-68451-042-9

Library of Congress Control Number: 2019956085

Published in the United States by
Salem Books
An imprint of Regnery Publishing
A division of Salem Media Group
300 New Jersey Ave NW
Washington, DC 20001
www.Regnery.com

Manufactured in the United States of America

10 9 8 7 6 5 4 3 2 1

Books are available in quantity for promotional or premium use. For information on discounts and terms, please visit our website: www.Regnery.com.

Contents

Foreword

I've always been the guy who leaves his annual checkup with a clean bill of health.

Until I wasn't.

Physical health and fitness have been a central theme of my life ever since childhood. In the elementary years, I would spend hours in the neighborhood playing football, basketball, capture the flag, kick the can, swimming, or riding bikes with the other kids.

In the early teen years, I would travel the state of Georgia year-round to play the junior tennis circuit. In between tournaments I would be on the court, drilling and practicing and pushing my body to its limits for an average of four hours per day.

In high school, I became a two-sport athlete and added the basketball court to the tennis court as part of my daily physical regimen.

In college, I spent more time on intramural sports than I did on academics. And since then, I have been to the gym almost every day getting the heart rate up, pumping iron, and eating healthy to stay fit and fight the aging process. My resting heart rate right now is forty-eight beats per minute, right alongside the Olympic long-distance runners.

All my life, doctors have been so complimentary of my physical health that one of them said, "It's people like you who could put people like me out of business."

That was two years ago.

But in the past year, several things started to go wrong. For the first time in my life I got some abnormal test results. Since then, I have been back to the lab so many times that I could walk its hallways blindfolded. The nurses and I know each other by name. For the first time in my life, I'm forced to face the fact that the mortality rate is one person per one person, including me. Someday and along with me, even Lebron James and Steph Curry and Serena Williams and Lindsey Vonn and Rafael Nadal will fade, and then they, too will expire. Indeed, none of us is exempted from the death toll of creation's groan.

So, it turns out that God gave me a Ford Escort for a body, not a Maserati. Since I turned fifty, it's as if the Escort has hit 100,000 miles and the warranty has expired and I suddenly find myself doing as much maintenance and repair as driving. To make matters worse, this earthen shell of a body is the only "car" God has given me to drive. I cannot replace it in this one life I've been given. And so, even though the coast is currently clear on my health, there are now three things, which might eventually become four things or even seven things or twenty things, that the doctors will need to watch closely for the rest of my days, until my days are done.

.

Why am I telling you these things? Because the things that are happening to my body are also the kinds of things that are happening over time to every person, every place, and everything. As far as we humans are concerned—whether mentally, emotionally, relationally, physically, or vocationally—we are all subject to what physicists refer to as the second law of thermodynamics. Every square inch of God's universe, and therefore every square inch of our lives, is gradually going to erode, fall apart, and flame out. The sun is losing energy by the day, the earth is becoming less inhabitable by the year, and like the grass and flowers of the field, we, too, are subject to the same sad trajectory.

Anne Lamott put it quite succinctly when asked what she thinks the world will be like one hundred years from now. Her answer was, "One hundred years? All new people."

These realities about the life we've been given to live, the people we are meant to live it with, and the world in which we find ourselves are bound to create fatigue and even despair for anyone whose eyes are open to the brokenness of everything but are not open to the power, promises, and covenantal care of God who alone can resolve and redeem the tension. Shakespeare's Macbeth summarizes this perspective accurately as he reflects on his wife's death: "Life is a tale told by an idiot, full of sound and fury and signifying nothing." Eventually, this idiot's tale becomes the central theme of life in a fallen world that does not recognize God, and that forgets both Him and His benefits.

But when God and His benefits do make their way into the picture, when the ring of the resurrected Christ comes home to us, saying, "Behold, I am making all things new," suddenly there is this other-worldly power—a cosmic gravitational force of sorts—that reorients our perspectives about broken people, broken places, and broken things. Beneath the banner of the resurrected Christ, we come to find that our current, broken lives are merely a middle chapter in the cosmic Story that God is writing. These middle chapters contain within them "many dangers, toils, and snares" through which we must travel. But through the eyes of faith, hope, and love, we come to understand even in the midst of them that these dangers, toils, and snares are only temporary afflictions—afflictions which, if we've been given the eyes of faith akin to the Apostle Paul, can be treated even as "light and momentary" because of what he called a "weight of glory beyond all comparison. For the things that are seen are transient, but the things that are unseen are eternal" (2 Corinthians 4:16-18).

Broken and Beloved is Sammy Rhodes's effort at awakening the eyes of our hearts, so that we too can begin to "see" those things that are, for now, unseen to us. It is a book that teaches us to frame God's Story—its rupture and its rapture, its tragedy and its triumph, its current, temporary chapters and its final, everlasting chapter—as an umbrella that is there to shelter and shade our own stories with the many dangers, toils, and snares that confront us. It is also the Story of a grace greater than every sorrow. It is a grace that will not only lead us home, but also sustain us with faith, hope, and love during the middle chapters.

You can trust Sammy's voice. Though he is young, he has seen and endured more than many who are twice his age. As these pages will reveal, he has known and carries with him the scars of disappointment, betrayal, depression, anxiety, social fear, addiction, cyber-bullying, and a tragic father wound. Indeed, the old soul that Sammy is has been birthed and trained and formed from the school of hardship and sorrow in his youth. Like Jesus our Lord, Sammy has learned faithfulness from a very early age, chiefly through the things that he has suffered (Hebrews 5:8).

One great thing about Sammy is that, amid the hardships of fallen life, he has also learned levity and joy and laughter. He is one of the funniest people I know. He is an outstanding and fiercely serious, yet hopeful, minister of the Gospel, especially with college students, among whom my own daughter is a current and direct and grateful beneficiary. When Sammy opens his mouth, people lean in to listen. When he speaks at conferences, his seminars are packed. I trust that as you read on, the reasons will be obvious to you.

In commending Sammy the author, it is a joy and privilege also to commend to you Sammy the man. I hope that *Broken and Beloved* will help you become more like Sammy. Specifically, I hope it helps you become more honest and real about the tragedies of life. And I hope it helps you become more hopeful about the God who made himself subject to, faithfully endured, died as a result of, was resurrected from, and is determined to reverse the curse of those very same tragedies.

Scott Sauls
Pastor of Christ Presbyterian Church and
author of *Jesus Outside the Lines* and *A Gentle Answer*

Introduction

I'm not a tattoo guy. I don't mean that I'm against them. Far from it. I mean that I've never had the confidence it takes to have one—at least one that doesn't look I lost a bet, got wasted on Jell-O shots and made a poor decision ... or a combination of the two. The older I get, the more convinced I am that there are only two kinds of people in the world: people who can pull off tattoos and people who should never be found within several miles of a tattoo parlor. I'm coming to terms with the fact that I'm the latter.

My wife, however, is a tattoo person, at least in the literal sense. On her twenty-first birthday she decided, as someone who was not a tattoo person, to shock the world in the form of a Japanese symbol meaning "Peace." I still envy the boldness of it. Tattoos are a permanent way of reminding others and ourselves that this is who we are. And even when we inevitably change, they are still ways of declaring that this is who I once was, what I was once like. There's a permanence to them that is powerful.

The prophet Isaiah knew something about this when he gave the people of God a powerful image about the Lord's love for them. "Behold, I have inscribed you on the palms of my hands." Take in that image for a second. Your name permanently inked in the Lord's hands. The hands that made the heavens, formed the earth, spread the seas, set the stars in the sky—those hands bear the marks of your name.

Those hands also bear the marks of our shame. They are nail-pierced hands: Jesus sits at the right hand of the Father, praying for those whose names are tattooed on His hands. Our names are inscribed in the wounds of the cross, the place where our brokenness and our belovedness meet. The place where our sin is no match for the grace of God. The place where our shame stands no chance against the mercy of God.

To bear our names is to bear our stories. It means the Lord meets us in particular ways, in particular places, with particular kindness, and with particular graces. This is why I have always been drawn to the Gospel of John. If the other gospel writers have a knack for details, John seems to have a knack for stories. If the others were journalists and historians, John is an artist. He weaves together these beautiful stories of Jesus meeting people in particular ways. Those stories always have two movements: the painful reality of their brokenness and the hopeful promise of what it means to be loved by Jesus.

If there is one theme woven throughout John's gospel and this book, it is that. We live in twin realities: we are broken, and we are beloved. We are broken by sin—our own sin, and that of others against us. I recently overheard someone at a coffee shop proudly declaring their lack of dating history—"At least I'm not damaged goods"—and my heart dropped. It took everything in me not to make my way to their table and gently tell them, "Friend, we're all damaged goods. It's just that some of us are damaged more obviously than others."

We're all damaged goods. We are formed in beauty, in majesty, in splendor. We are made in God's image, and wonderfully so. Yet we are a glorious ruin. Like the ruins of an ancient temple, the beauty is evident—yet so are the marks of our disrepair. Some of us feel our brokenness keenly while some of us hide it with great performance, but it is there, and the cracks are showing. Humpty Dumpty was not alone in his great fall. We are broken. Who can put us together again?

This is precisely what Jesus has come to do. What all the king's horses and all the king's men could not: to put us together again. This is what Jesus is doing in the Gospel of John, which is why John opens with an overture harking back to Genesis, to creation. Where the fall has ruined God's creation, Jesus has come to recreate. He has come to bear our brokenness with great love. He has come to carry the stories of our shame in the wounds of His cross.

He is God's Beloved Son, yet at the cross He is broken for our sin. He bears two names on our behalf: Broken and Beloved. This means His work in our lives is to bear witness to those twin realities. Yes, we are more broken than we know, much less care to believe or dare to admit. And, yes, we are more loved than we could possibly imagine. To be loved is the cry of our hearts. To be broken is the reality of our lives. To be loved in the face of our brokenness is the healing we have found in Jesus.

My prayer is that this book would be a witness to both of these realities in your own life. I hope that in it you can see something of your own brokenness. I hope, too, you can begin to grasp your belovedness as well. To be loved by Jesus is to grow in your grasp of both realities. You are broken, yet you are beloved.

Maybe I've finally found my tattoo. Or tattoos, I should say. "Broken" on one side, and "Beloved" on the other. Whether or not I ever get them, they remain true about me. I am a broken man, and yet I am a man who is greatly loved. I get to sing, with tears in my eyes and truth in my heart, "My name is graven on his hands. My name is written on his heart. I know that while in Heaven he stands, no tongue can bid me thence depart."[1] Yes, I am broken. But, oh yes, I am loved. Because the Beloved was broken for me, I am finally free. Free to confess my brokenness to Him, and free to rest in the grasp of His love. After all, He holds me with nail-pierced hands that bear the mark of my name. Yours, too.

May the chapters of this book bless your life to this end as we learn what it means to be broken and beloved together.

Sincerely,
Sammy
March 2020

CHAPTER 1

A World of Brokenness

"And the Word became flesh and dwelt among us, and we have seen his glory, glory as of the only Son from the Father, full of grace and truth."

John 1:14 (ESV)

"The Word became flesh and moved into the neighborhood."

Eugene Peterson[1]

"Aren't you, like me, hoping that some person, thing, or event will come along to give you that final feeling of inner well-being you desire?"

Henri Nouwen[2]

"And did you get what you wanted from this life, even so?
I did.
And what did you want?
To call myself beloved,
to feel myself
beloved on the earth."

Wallace Stevens[3]

I was fourteen years old when I met Jesus, and my world lay crumbled at my awkward teenage feet, of which I was very self-consciously ashamed. The Rhodeses have many distinctive qualities, and one I (evidently) inherited is the way both of my big toes curve into my other four toes like they've had too much to drink and keep falling into them. They were such a cause of shame to me that when an older babysitter, the kind that make emerging teenage boys suddenly discover that they are emerging teenage boys, had just a year before seen them on accident, I stopped speaking to her entirely. She had seen what, at thirteen, I imagined was the ugliest part of me. She had seen the Hyde to my Jekyll. The Gollum to my Smeagol. *At the beach, by the pool, during gym at school, I do not want them to see my feet, I will not, I shall not, I cannot show them the defeat that are my bent and broken feet.* Sometimes I wish Dr. Seuss wrote nursery rhymes for the awkwardness that is our teenage years.

At fourteen, my feet had not magically changed, and my world was still crumbled beneath them. My dad had not come home. At ten, I should have known that things weren't looking good when he moved out of the house for a few long months. But at ten, my biggest concerns were which

Transformer to buy next: Bumblebee or Firescream? Or which set of baseball cards: Upper Deck or Fleer? Or which pack of gum: Big League Chew or Hubba Bubba?

There isn't room in your preteen mind to comprehend a marriage falling apart, a parent coming apart at the seams from addiction. But at fourteen, it had all begun to come to a head. Dad had been caught with another woman. Again. But this time, things were more serious because he had also begun dabbling in crack cocaine, which, if you know anything about crack, doesn't let you simply dabble. By fourteen, the dabbling had gone from part-time entertainment to full-time addiction. By fourteen, Dad had left home and left behind a cloud of questions that had gathered suddenly, like a dark summer storm. Why didn't he just come home? Was it because he, like me, couldn't stand the sight of my feet?

How old were you the first time you realized that the world was broken, that *you* were broken, beyond your ability to fix it? This was that moment for me. Not that I could work it out emotionally, much less theologically, but I knew, in my bones, that the world was not as it should be. That married couples should do their best to stay together, and not just for the children. That parents should do their best to stay in the picture, however imperfectly. That our bodies should be kept in honor and our brains with a decent fill of dopamine. That we should not lose a loved one, ever, to the hell of addiction. That children should not be worried about money or food or housing or their family being torn apart.

How old were you when you realized that everything is not awesome (sorry, *Lego Movie*), but that everything is broken? That life so often feels like stepping on scattered Legos in the dark of the night, in its pain and in its surprise? I don't say this because I'm a Type Four on the Enneagram and love focusing on the darker side of life. I say this as someone who genuinely believes that, if our eyes are open, we can see brokenness happening all around us, as well as within us, all the time. Everything is broken, ourselves most of all.

A Broken World

Maybe your first experience of brokenness was simply living in a world that often is not as it should be. You heard your parents speak in hushed whispers about a tragic event like 9/11 or a mass shooting that seems to happen almost every other day now. You flip through the TV or scroll through your phone, and everyone is talking about the latest political scandal, the latest revelation of sexual abuse, or the latest racially motivated hate crime. It doesn't take living in this world very long before you come up against something in the world that, as best you understand it, is cause for heartache or at least genuine concern.

I recently watched a documentary about the ongoing water crisis in Flint, Michigan, which is still affecting so many lives. Through a failure in leadership, short-sighted business dealings, and straight-up greed, an entire inner city has been poisoned with a dangerous water supply. The water has become toxic, completely undrinkable. To make matters worse, no one seems willing to own or address the situation. It seems to be the perfect storm of a broken system leading to a broken reality for so many people, especially underprivileged families in the poorer parts of the city.

Only once in my life have I ever worried about drinking local water: in a remote part of Peru, where most locals live in Third World conditions. Clean water has always been a given for me, as it has for most of us. Sometimes I wonder, given the ongoing brokenness in a place like Flint, if someone called and offered me a job there tomorrow, would I take it? If I'm being honest, it would be a quick no. My justification would be how dangerous it would be for my family, how foolish it would be to take them to a place that might lead to their harm. Maybe I would lie and say I would pray about it, but ultimately, the god of my comfort would speak to me.

This is why I love the way Eugene Peterson translates John 1:14: "Love came down and moved into the neighborhood." It takes everything in me not to cross the street when I cross paths with the homeless, and yet Jesus draws near to the broken. Jesus enters into broken places unashamedly. He moves into the neighborhood of our broken world. He isn't passing through. He has come to fully and finally mend all that is broken. He has left the comforts of Heaven to make a home with the afflicted.

Growing up, *Mr. Rogers' Neighborhood* was an important part of my childhood. There was something about watching Mr. Rogers that felt like home should be. He would walk through that door, slip off his jacket and ease into his cardigan, then swap out his stiff dress shoes to lace up his comfortable sneakers, and I felt immediately at ease. A man of authority drawing near with comfort and kindness. It felt like everything a father should be.

With a smile on his face, he didn't shirk from the hard realities of the world. Instead, he sought to explain them, as best he could, to children who were frightened, who felt alone in a world that is often downright scary. Recently in the documentary made about his life, he was shown in an interview speaking about his life's purpose, which was, in his words, to tell children that "they are loved and capable of loving." He sought to be a beacon of love in a world full of hate. A light, however small, shining in the darkness.

In this way, Mr. Rogers is a glimpse into the heart of Jesus. Jesus moves into the neighborhood not simply to show us what Love looks like as it sits with us, eats with us, laughs with us, and cries with us. He moved into the neighborhood to show us that He isn't just passing through until He moves up the ladder to something better, somewhere more beautiful. He is committed to this broken place, to spend His life, both on Earth and in Heaven, making sure it is fully and finally mended. This broken world we call home is now the neighborhood of Jesus.

A Broken Situation

Or maybe, like me, it was not so much what was happening in the world around you that woke you to the reality of brokenness but more what was happening in your life or home at the moment. A messy divorce, a sudden death, a diagnosis of cancer, or an experience of abuse can all easily be a window into a world that is not as it should be. People fail us. Life fails us. It feels as if God fails us. They deal us a bad hand, and it feels like the deck is stacked against us.

The same year my dad left home, I also lost a friend to suicide. His name was Jamie, and we were actually distant cousins. We grew up playing basketball together. We spent the night at each others' houses. I loved spending the night at Jamie's because his mom would make desserts that would've made Paula Deen jealous. Then she would let us play flashlight freeze tag well past our bedtime. Jamie had a big heart and an even bigger mischievous kind of smile. I can still hear him call me "Cuz."

Then one day, I woke up for school in seventh grade, and there was the kind of tense quietness in our house where you know in your soul that something has gone terribly wrong. My mom broke the news to me. Jamie had shot himself. They weren't sure if it was an accident or intentional, but Jamie didn't make it through. Counselors descended on our school that morning, a flock of well-meaning strangers, to make sure we were OK. My friends were not OK. We were not OK. I was not OK. How can you lose someone you love to a death and be "OK"?

The first moment I really began wrestling with Jesus happened shortly after Jamie's death. My friends were telling about their youth pastor (who would later become a father figure to me) and something he had said about the book of Job, specifically about that enigmatic passage where Satan comes before God and asks permission to tempt God's servant Job to disobedience and despair. "Does Job really love You, or does he just love this nice life of health and wealth You've given him?" God allows Satan to wreak havoc. To turn Job's life, his world, upside down overnight. He takes every single thing near to Job's heart from him. His children. His wealth. His health. The scope of Job's suffering is unimaginable.

Job's counselors show up and, like a bad conservative news blogger, tell Job all this brokenness happening around him is his fault. He must have done something, *something*, for God to allow all this horrible suffering to befall him. Job stays quiet. His friends don't know the hell that has been Job's life of late, nor do they know what they're talking about. Like Pharisees so often do, they add to Job's pain and suffering instead of easing it. And that's why God rebukes them so harshly for their presumptive speaking of things they don't know when all that was needed was compassionate listening.

Then Job begins to speak his confusion, anger, doubt, and fears to God. And in his Psalm-like speech, he says something striking: "I know that in my flesh I shall see God." In the brokenness of his situation, he is clinging to something, namely the character of this God he knows and loves and serves. God alone has the right to give and to take away. Yes. But more. He cares. He is not immune to our pain, or removed from our suffering. That somehow, *somehow*, He will get involved.

Then John writes, "the Word became flesh," and something better than Job hoped for comes to fruition. "I know that in my flesh I shall see God," but better: "I know that I shall see God in my flesh." The Son of God taking on our flesh in all its frailty, moving into a life so tender, so fragile, that suffering and death are daily realities. In Jesus, we see God in our flesh—entering our broken world, yes, but also entering into our broken situations, whatever they might be. The Psalmist says, "He knows our frame, remembering that we are but dust." He does indeed know our frame. He shares it.

A Broken Self

I still don't love my feet, but I have come to accept them. I realize now, at thirty-nine, that my feet were a metaphor for the brokenness I was feeling. I couldn't have articulated it then, but there was a part of me that felt deeply that, for my life to go so wrong, something must be wrong with me. I know I'm not alone in the feeling. It's the feeling that maybe if I weren't so broken, I could somehow control the brokenness around me.

The problem is that I am broken goods, and so are you. I don't say that to run either one of us down. I say that because that is a fundamental truth of what it means to be a sinner. I am both a victim and a villain. I have experienced wrongs done to me and against me. I have also wronged and hurt others often throughout my life. Both of these things are true about me. You and I are both victim and villain. This means we need both truth and grace.

In other words, we need, on the one hand, an Advocate. Someone who pleads for justice to be done on our behalf. Someone who seeks to protect us, defend us. Someone unafraid to go to battle for us against all who would seek us harm. Someone who embodies Micah 6:8: who does justice, loves mercy, and walks humbly with God.

No one has embodied this more beautifully in recent years than Rachel Denhollander. First, she bravely shared her own story of sexual abuse at the hands of Dr. Larry Nassar, an Olympic trainer who used his position of power and privilege to prey on hundreds of innocent young women and girls, all in the name of "medical procedure."

Rachel has become an advocate for all of these precious sisters who experienced the horror of abuse that she experienced. She began calling out the abuse, taking legal action, using every gift at her disposal to fight for victims. In this way, Rachel gives us a glimpse into the heart of Jesus, fiercely full of truth. Jesus Himself knows what it is to be a victim. Jesus has a heart to draw near and fiercely defend His precious brothers and sisters from their abusers, who want to call evil good and good evil.

Jesus also has a heart that is full of grace. Not a grace that excuses sin, but a grace that cleanses it. A grace that says, "I know who you are, I know what you've done. It is worse than you know, and it is precisely why I have come." It is a grace that sees us at our worst yet loves us at God's best. A grace that, in the words of Charles Wesley, is greater than all our sin.

A Broken Savior

One of my very favorite movies is a '90s animated film called *The Iron Giant*. It takes place at the height of the cold war between the USA and the USSR. In it, a young fatherless boy named Hogarth happens upon a strange scene. He's playing war in the woods near an electrical plant when suddenly a huge object falls onto the plant from the sky. Hogarth can see the sparks begin to fly, electrocuting this giant metal object, until he runs over to shut off the power. There Hogarth meets the Iron Giant, and a friendship is forged.

As their friendship begins, so does the fear of a general in the US Army. He has heard rumors of a giant robot roaming the town and assumes it must be some kind of Soviet spy. He calls for reinforcement from every branch of the military. The movie builds toward the dramatic closing scene where the crazed general and a cavalry of military backup chase the Giant into the heart of town. It is there that the fearful general, without thinking, fires a nuclear missile meant to destroy the Giant without realizing that it will also destroy every person in town.

As the missile soars into the sky, the Giant takes one look at the people—and then looks at his friend, Hogarth. Suddenly, he takes flight into the sky, and as he reaches the edge of the atmosphere, he grabs the missile, takes it upon himself, and is destroyed into a thousand pieces. Just before he sacrifices himself, he smiles.

Tim Keller recalls watching this scene and thinking of Hebrews 12, where the author says, "For the joy set before him, Jesus endured the cross, despising its shame." Keller then asks, "What was His joy? His joy was you. His joy was me."[4] His joy was entering into our broken world, our broken situation, our broken lives, and taking that brokenness upon himself that we might become whole. The Beloved was broken so that everyone who feels broken might become the beloved of God. That is the joy of Jesus.

The truth is that our brokenness is real, and there's nothing we can do about it. There is an honest despair in admitting that fact. But there is a still, small hope that yet whispers to our despair. Someone has moved into the neighborhood, full of truth and grace, and He can do something about it. His name is Broken and Beloved. He is the one who says, "This is my body broken for you." And He is the Beloved Son of God, with whom the Father is well pleased. His brokenness is our healing. His belovedness is our hope.

The other night, my daughter came to me with a strange request: "Dad, show me your feet."

"What? Why?" I asked.

"Mom says I have your feet."

So I took off my socks, made sure the smell wasn't too awful, and put my foot right next to hers. I told her, "See how the big toe curves in. That's just a Rhodes foot." She smiled, not sure exactly what to say, but hopefully feeling a little less alone.

I met Jesus at fourteen, and for the last twenty-five years, He has been leading me into my new name. When I met Him, there was a song that became sweet to me, "I Will

Change Your Name." I still remember sitting in the front seat of my mom's car, hearing the words for the first time. "I will change your name. You shall no longer be called Wounded, Outcast, Lonely, or Afraid. I will change your name. Your new name shall be: Confidence, Joyfulness, Overcoming One, Faithfulness, Friend of God, One who seeks My face."

He didn't change my circumstances, but He did change my name. My first name is still Broken. This side of Heaven, I will grow, I have grown, but I will never be perfect, never be free of sin or flaws. I will still face loneliness and fear. I still bear the scars of life in a broken world.

But I have a new last name, with more distinctive traits than the ones found in the Rhodes family line: Beloved. One so precious to Jesus that He didn't just pass through my life. He moved into the neighborhood. He plans on building a life of love with you and me forever. We can stop looking at our feet and walk with Him as those who, even though broken, are forever beloved.

CHAPTER 2

The Wine Always Runs Out

"Everyone serves the good wine first, and when people have drunk freely, then the poor wine. But you have kept the good wine until now."

John 2:10 (ESV)

"But Jesus came to renew all things, to change our broken humanity into a new unity as he changed the water into wine. If he brings the disciples first of all to a wedding feast, it is not only to affirm the importance and beauty of the bonding of man and woman in the oneness of human sexuality, but also to reveal to his disciples and to each one of us the deepest thirst in us: our desire and need to love and be loved."

Jean Vanier[1]

"Daddy needs a drink to calm down the badness, to execute his gladness on the fullness of his cup / Daddy needs a drink to keep the wheels from rubbing, to compensate for nothing, or nothing going on"

Drive By Truckers[2]

"Love is that liquor sweet, and most divine, that my God feels as blood, but I as wine."

George Herbert[3]

The first time I ever got proper drunk, it was a sad affair. I was a senior in college and a late bloomer, as they say. I grew up an Episcopalian, so trust me when I say alcohol was around like sweet tea at a Southern Baptist fellowship potluck. Instead of buckets of fried chicken, there were iced buckets full of beer. But I met Jesus at fourteen, and the one way I knew to follow Him was not to mess around with peppermint schnapps like the wild pagans in the grade above me. I was a bit of a legalist about it—but more of that to come in a later chapter.

By my senior year of college, I had joined a fraternity. I never saw myself joining a fraternity, mainly because, in my mind, that was the last thing a good youth group kid does when he goes to college. But the Lord works in mysterious ways, as they say, and by the end of sophomore year, I was lonely, had just gone through a painful breakup, and, quite honestly, just needed some friends. A guy I knew from high school said my roommate and I should join, so we did.

Which brings me to the first night I ever got proper drunk. I wanted to know what it felt like. Still too proud to let my friends see me make an obvious mistake, I went to the local liquor store alone, bought a liter of Captain Morgan, went back to my room, shut the door, poured a stadium cup full, and set sail on the high seas of getting a horrible case of the spins. I don't recommend it. Sailing with the Captain left me worse than seasick.

I don't know what your relationship has been like with alcohol, but I do know that for many of us, that relationship can get complicated. Scripture speaks of the way it can gladden the heart, but it is also honest about the way it can dull the senses and quench the Spirit's work in our lives. "Do not get drunk with wine, but be filled with the Spirit." It's a strange combination of words, as if Paul knew well the temptation implicit in drinking, how it offers an escape from life rather than a Spirit-led embrace of it.

So why is wine at the centerpiece of Jesus's first miracle? Not just cheap two-buck chuck, but the kind of wine that stops a man whose job is to recommend wine dead in his tracks? This sommelier is blown away by how incredible this wine is. Jesus makes a wine that this couple could not possibly have hoped to afford. And He does it not that they would believe in the wine but that they would believe in Him.

Players Gonna Play, Couples Gonna Fight

It's interesting that the first miracle of Jesus is smack-dab in the middle of a couple's fight. These newlyweds have barely said their vows, and you can already cut the tension with a butter knife, the bamboo kind you find in fancy bakeries. How is it that they had already run out of wine? Who messed up? The bride or the groom? Or was it their families? The best man? Why had the wine run out? John doesn't tell us. But what he doesn't have to tell us is what it's like to be in the middle of a fight with your significant other.

A few years ago, my wife and I took our kids to the beach. It's actually one of my very favorite beaches in the world: Pawley's Island, South Carolina. It's where I went after that painful break-up in college when a concerned friend invited me to get out of town and spend some time there. It was there that I experienced bioluminescence for the first time, that common miracle of wet sand lighting up like stars when you step on it. It was like the true and better "Footprints" poem, without all the cheesy sentiment. It was there the Lord dragged my stubborn self as I fought to hold onto a failed relationship. It was there the Lord reminded me of His steadfast faithfulness even in the face of my steadfast foolishness.

It is also the beach where I proposed to my wife. That same spot where I first experienced bioluminescence became the spot where I dropped to one knee, pulled out the ring I had awkwardly stuffed into my jacket pocket, and popped the question. My Enneagram Six wife's first words, I kid you not, were "Who knows about this?" said more with fearful force than romantic tenderness. It's part of what I still love so much about her. I never have to wonder what she's thinking or what she's afraid of.

But this particular time at Pawley's was a stressful one. I had just gone through a traumatic experience but was having difficulty actually talking about it. So instead, as a good older millennial, I blogged about it. My wife stressed too, mainly because she was unsure of how to help me with my stress, not to mention the stress of raising four children under the age of nine, and had miraculously somehow not found the time to read said blogs. So as we stepped through the condominium doors, the first words out of my mouth were, "You don't love me. You didn't even read my blogs!"

Five years later, I can hear how ridiculous it sounds. Really? The woman who has been with you for well over a decade, shared a bed, mothered your children, seen the awful way you can leave a bathroom—not to mention a kitchen—doesn't know you? But fights don't work in a logical way. They are dripping with emotion that leaks out of the painful places of our lives like an upstairs bathroom that has started leaking into the kitchen. How can you stop it? Where is the leak coming from?

This tendency we have is like one first seen in our forefather and -mother, Adam and Eve. The whole garden is theirs, but suddenly there is a disruption. And the fingers that had just been locked in sweet embrace are now pointed, like a trusted firearm, at the other, aimed and ready to fire. Their nakedness, once a point of deep intimacy, is now a cause of deep shame. Their words, once used to build up one another in love, are now being used to tear each other down. That is, until God steps in and covers their shame, transforming a nearby animal Adam has just named into skins for new clothes to cover the nakedness of their shame.

The Wine Always Runs Out

I don't remember too much from the night of our wedding rehearsal dinner. Weddings are often like that. You plan and you plan and you plan, and then the big weekend comes and goes like a flash of lightning in the night sky. But I do remember one toast. It was by my father-in-law. He was a wine connoisseur and brought one of his most prized bottles, an older Silver Oak cabernet sauvignon. He stood up, held up the bottle, and said to me and my wife, "May your marriage be like a good bottle of wine. Better and better the older it gets."

I've always loved that line. "Better and better the older it gets." That's not the way marriage always goes. Often our marriages sour over time. The stresses of life, mixed with our inability to patiently build intimacy together, create a recipe of bitterness and a dissatisfaction that grows like a fungus around the trunk of an old tree. Time, instead of healing the wounds we inflict on each other, causes those wounds to open so wide they eventually swallow us whole.

It doesn't take being married very long to realize the wine always runs out. I don't mean that we grow quickly tired of one another, although ask any couple who's been married for a while if they knew exactly what they were getting themselves into. I often say to the couples I marry that I'm not a big believer in premarital counseling, but I am a huge believer in post-marital counseling. Because none of us goes into marriage with eyes wide open. You can't. Everything up until your wedding day has been a job interview, but you don't how someone really works until they're on the clock.

Not to mention how often we change. This person you're saying "I do" to today will be in many ways a completely different person a year from now, three years from now, ten years from now. I've always loved the way that Lewis Smedes put it: "My wife has been married to five different men, and all of them are me." Your vow is less a transaction, more a promise. A way of saying "I will be here for you no matter the ways you grow and change and fail."

The wine always runs out. People change. Circumstances change. Money changes. Sex changes. Houses change. Jobs change. Family dynamics change. Or worse, they never change. Children change everything. You change. Life is rarely static. It can't be controlled or pinned down neatly into the latest spiraled Lily Pulitzer calendar. John Lennon famously said, "Life is what happens when you're busy making other plans." We could also say life is what happens when your best-made plans are suddenly cancelled, and unless you're an introvert, this is not the life you hoped for.

Turning thirty has been the hardest birthday for me yet. Not because the day itself was bad. My wife is an incredible gift giver and had orchestrated the loved ones in our lives to pool funds together and buy me a first-generation iPad. When my wife turned thirty a year and a half before, the only gift she got from me was a book, and it wasn't even a good one. Remember when *Jon and Kate Plus Eight* was a show we watched? Remember when Kate wrote a book about their lives together? Remember when I ran down at the last minute to the local Books-a-Million and got my wife the saddest thirtieth birthday present of all time? No gift would probably have been better than *that* gift. At least we can laugh about it now. But every now and again, I see a small tear start gathering in one of my wife's eyes as we laugh about it. It's hard being married to someone who thinks a reality TV star's book makes an acceptable thirtieth birthday present.

When I turned thirty, though, it was like I suddenly woke up in my life and wasn't sure what had happened. *Was this the life I wanted, or did I just go along with it because I hate confrontation?* I kept thinking this stupid thought. When John Calvin turned thirty, he had already written *The Institutes.* When Bob Dylan turned thirty, he had already written several music-altering albums. Why I thought of these two men specifically only makes sense if you've spent any time in the world of Presbyterianism. But I couldn't shake the feeling that somehow life had not turned into what it was supposed to. And thirty, for some reason, was the expiration date. Here I was with a beautiful wife, three amazing kids, an incredible job, but for some stupid reason I couldn't taste it. The wine flowed, yet it felt as if the wine had run out. I could almost hear the prophet Jeremiah (another success before thirty, probably) say those words from the Lord, "They have forsaken me, the fountain of living waters, and hewed out cisterns from themselves, broken cisterns that can hold no water."

Jesus Makes the Best Wine

In the same way that His Father showed up in the garden to cover the shame of a couple, so Jesus shows up at the beginning of this couple's life together and follows His Father's lead. Jesus—in quiet, hidden ways—shows them that the waters of shame they swim in are no match for the wine of His grace. The wine always runs out. That's the bad news. But the good news is this: Jesus makes the best wine.

Why does Jesus perform his first miracle at a wedding? Maybe it's because there are few relationships that are better signposts to the world of the grace of God we find in Christ. Over the last thirteen years of ministry, the request I get the most when it comes to weddings is that I would preach the Gospel clearly. I love that request. Preaching the Gospel at a wedding is so much fun.

But I always tell the couple something I hope they take to heart: "I will gladly preach the Gospel with as much clarity and force as I can on your wedding day. But I want you to know that your marriage is a far more powerful Gospel presentation than any sermon I could ever preach. The way you bear with one another patiently, through thick and thin. The way you meet each other with astounding forgiveness in the face of deep hurts and sins. The way you walk with each other through the inevitable suffering and disappointments of life. That will show your loved ones far more about the good news of Jesus than my sermon could even hope to do."

I've always loved the way N. T. Wright puts it: "Marriage is hilarious; laugh with it. Marriage is solemn and serious;

stand in awe of it. Marriage is hard work; get on with it. Marriage is a celebration: drink to it. Marriage is a gift: thank God for it. Marriage is a signpost: raise that signpost and maintain it for the rest of us, for the rest of the world. The hour has come. God has kept the best wine till now. Eat, friends, drink, and be drunk with love."[4]

But Jesus is doing something else besides honoring God's beautiful Gospel design for our marriages. He is also showing us something about Himself. Jesus begins His public ministry at a wedding because He has come as the Bridegroom. He is the One who has been moved by love to enter into an everlasting covenant with us. And He has come with eyes wide open. He is highly aware of our flaws. He knows of our unfaithfulness and has felt it. He is no stranger to our foolish and fickle hearts. But that doesn't deter Him even for a second. He has come to marry us and spend the rest of His life devoted to our flourishing.

A few years ago, some married friends of ours were going through a hard time in their marriage. The husband was gone for work a lot, and quite honestly, he found more satisfaction at his job than he did at home. His wife had taken notice. Overwhelmed by the struggles of parenting and a husband who she felt barely noticed her anymore, she turned to an old friend, wine. It started slowly. Polishing off a bottle a night. Then two. Her husband, whose affection was elsewhere at the moment, didn't notice at first. Until one night he came home and found his wife passed out, several bottles of wine collected around her feet. It was a wake-up call.

Jesus is at His best when things are falling apart, it seems. This married couple did what you do when you're afraid you've ruined your marriage forever: they asked for help. Through the love and support of good friends and good counseling, their marriage has not only been brought back from the dead but has found new life in surprising and encouraging ways. The wine always runs out. But Jesus is still able to make the best wine. He can take the mundane and make it not only better but spectacularly so. He can take the old and make it new. As Paul Miller, reflecting on John 2, likes to say, "When Jesus shows up to a party, it doesn't just keep going. It gets better."[5]

Jesus doesn't just make the best wine, He *is* the best wine. Which is why He has told His betrothed that He has gone before them into the heavenly country, our forever home, and He is there building a home for us to come and enjoy with Him forever. A home where the life of love He has started with us here will go on forever.

But more than that. Jesus points our hearts to the best wedding reception the world has ever known. A wedding reception that will make Kate and William's or Meghan and Harry's look boring. He calls it the Marriage Supper of the Lamb. There, communion will become a literal feast in the presence of Jesus, a feast He paid for with His own body and blood. It is the feast every delicious meal we've ever tasted anticipates. It is the reception every one of our lonely hearts has longed for. "He takes a poor vile sinner into his house of wine."

There's a song by an old Christian band called Waterdeep called "Both of Us Will Feel the Blast." In it, they envision what that celebration meal will be like.

I hope we sit together when Jesus serves the wine,
so I can look into your eyes when I taste it the first time.
And I know there's no secrets when you're sitting at that table,
but I believe we'll smile real knowingly when we read the label,
and it says "passion sacrificed to keep from going crazy."
We'll tip our glasses to the Host who used to look so hazy,
and drink it down all sweet and slow and slip inside His mind.
And realize as it goes down this is communion wine.
This is communion wine.[6]

The wine of all the earthly things we have ever put our hope in always runs out. But at the Marriage Supper of the Lamb, the wine never runs out because the Lamb is the Wine. He promises to be with us forever. He is keeping the best wine until last. Truly, our cup does overflow. It overflows with the wine of Jesus's grace to us. Let us drink and be drunk with His love.

CHAPTER 3

Our Need for Grace

"Nicodemus said to him, 'How can these things be?' Jesus answered him, 'Are you the teacher of Israel and yet you do not understand these things?'"

John 3:9–10 (ESV)

"All human nature vigorously resists grace because grace changes us and the change is painful."

Flannery O'Connor[1]

"Our worst days are never so bad that you are beyond the reach of God's grace. And your best days are never so good that you are beyond the need of God's grace."

Jerry Bridges[2]

"What do you need? Tell the group what you need."

If there was a countdown of the top ten most uncomfortable moments of my life, this would easily be in my top three. I sat there, statuesque, palms sweaty, but not in the Eminem-about-to-kill-a-rap-battle kind of way. The person asking the question was our counselor, trying to lead this scared group of men out of the darkness of sexual addiction and into the light of real intimacy and connection. Her question has stayed with me: What do I need? Why am I still so afraid to talk about my needs? Why do I treat the word "need" like it is my sworn enemy?

There are two dynamics that make this question so hard. The first: do I even know what I really need right now? Am I in touch with my own heart in a way that I can hear and understand its shouts and cries, aches and tears, hopes and fears? The second: am I willing to risk making the secrets of my heart known to all? Or at least known to a select group of friends or family who are able and willing to do the same with me?

As I sat in an infuriatingly beige room that night, pounding LifeSavers Wint-O-Greens like they were a basket of McDonald's fries, I'm not sure I was capable of doing either.

In John 3, we meet a man named Nicodemus who everyone esteemed as a good man. The kind of man who, with an impressive academic and theological resume and an even more impressive moral resume, commanded respect and attention. A Billy Graham of Jerusalem, but with a Harvard pedigree. A man who was outwardly impressive and seemingly sincere. A man perfectly comfortable in both the teaching hall and the board room of his day. A man who had not yet begun to grapple with his need for grace.

Our Need for Grace

Nicodemus in many ways would make the perfect Southern gentleman. It's very clear that he's a good man. He's the leading Jewish teacher in all of Israel, which would be the equivalent of being the chair of the religion department at a Duke or a Harvard. He's polished and nice, with an impeccable resume, both academically and spiritually. He's well-respected. Kids in the neighborhood want to be him. He's been on the cover of *Time*, maybe *Garden and Gun* too. He's successful. But there's one thing Jesus says he isn't: Born again.

Now that phrase could conjure up all kinds of things, depending on your background. Let me deconstruct the religious baggage you may have around it. It might conjure an image for you of backward, conservative, Bible-belty Christianity. The kind that says things like, "I don't cuss, drink, or chew, or go with girls who do." That's not what Jesus is advocating. In fact, that's the kind of moralism that Jesus has come to undo.

Or it might bring to mind for you the overly emotional youth-group experiences, the kind that led you to give your life to Jesus twenty times, never being quite sure you felt it enough or were on fire enough or whatever [insert new hip Christian phrase of your choosing here] enough. Being born again has much less to do with feelings than actual (slow) transformation.

You can actually translate the Greek phrase Jesus uses in two ways: born again or born from above. John loves to use words and phrases that have two meanings, *double entendres* that have twofold significance and application. The phrase here is pretty simple: *it's being made new from the inside out.*

The Old Testament prophet Ezekiel pictured new birth in two different ways. One is a pile of bones lying lifeless on the ground, and suddenly God breathes into them, and they take flesh and muscle and begin dancing. The other is a man with a stone heart, and God does a radically invasive surgery where He takes out the dead, cold heart of stone and gives the man a beating, blood-pumping heart of flesh.

The apostle Paul expounds on this idea from Jesus in Ephesians 2 when he says that before we experience God making us alive, making us new, we are like spiritual zombies, dead in our sins and still walking around. What a zombie needs isn't to be taken to J. Crew to pick out a new outfit, then taken to an upscale barbershop for a fresh, hipster fade, and finally off to a trendy salon for a mani/pedi. What a zombie needs is for someone to come and make it human again from the inside out.

There's a way of doing Christianity that's more like giving a zombie a makeover than it is like dead people being made alive, broken people being made new.

This is why I'm convinced that Satan loved the old WB TV show *7th Heaven* way more than the dark AMC show *Breaking Bad*. *7th Heaven*, if you remember it, was a show full of nice people being nice. There was actually an episode where Reverend Camden deals with his youngest daughter, Ruthie, about her gum addiction. A far cry from the soul-twisting journey of Walter White from nice high school science teacher to deranged and scarily evil meth lord. *7th Heaven* was a nice, safe family show. No cussing. Nice, clean-cut moral principles. "Problems" of the gum-addiction variety. It made you feel good and want to be a better person. The problem was that, in the hundreds of episodes that always concluded with a tidbit of a Reverend Cameron sermon, the name Jesus Christ was never once mentioned. When there is no real sin to repent of, there is no need for a real Savior. Walter White, on the other hand, even though he never used the word "sin," knew something of his need to be miraculously forgiven and delivered of the ways he was destroying the lives of everyone he ever loved, as well as his own.

This is why when Presbyterian preacher Donald Grey Barnhouse once preached through the book of Romans and talked about that verse in the third chapter where Paul says no one is good, not one, he must have shocked his congregation. Barnhouse said if Satan were to take over an entire city, it wouldn't be like what we would think. Instead, Barnhouse preached, "All of the bars would be closed, pornography banished, and pristine streets would be filled with tidy pedestrians who smiled at each other. There would be no swearing. The children would say, 'Yes, sir' and 'No, ma'am,' and churches would be full every Sunday ... where Christ is not preached."[3]

What Barnhouse meant was that Christians aren't good, moral people. They are desperately bad people who have looked to Jesus for grace. This means that to be a Christian is to be made suddenly aware of your need for Christ to save you, like a baby being born into the world is suddenly aware of his need to be cared for and fed and clothed and held by his parents. The saddest thing in the world is a toddler who doesn't think he needs his parents. Even sadder is the teenager who thinks he's better than his parents. How much more so with God? To be a Christian is to be a needy baby who cries out for help. Or a teenager who knows that his parents are far wiser than him and won't give up on him. But who of us likes to be seen as needy?

This humble recognition of need is what Nicodemus can't believe. Why? Because it means all the things he's worked so hard for and all the things he's put down on his spiritual resume to commend himself to God mean absolutely nothing at the end of the day. Because it means that all that matters at the end of the day is for him to recognize his need for Christ and to trust Christ to provide everything he needs.

This is why I love the story of what a campus ministry in London did years ago to welcome students. They set up signs all over a campus that simply said, "Only bad people go to Heaven." I love to imagine the confused faces of hungover students doing a double take at the words. This ministry knew what Nicodemus didn't yet know: Jesus didn't come for the healthy but for the sick. He didn't come for the squeaky clean but for those, like Walter White, who have made a mess of their lives.

The Mystery of Grace

The natural next question is this: how does one receive this new birth? What does grace look like when it comes? How does it begin to change the direction of our thinking, our loving, our lives? This is where Jesus really emphasizes something else: That God's life-changing grace is as unpredictable as the wind—yet as visibly powerful too. In other words, it's something beyond our control that completely turns our lives upside down. The Spirit's work in making people new, Jesus says, is sudden and mysterious. It's unpredictable and powerful.

Think about your own conversion for a moment, if you've experienced it yet. You may be able to point to a specific day, maybe even an hour. Your experience was really dramatic. Or perhaps it was more gradual. You can't point to a day and time, but rather an unfolding series of smaller moments where Jesus became a little more beautiful, a little more believable brought you to Him. The door of grace began to crack, however slightly, and its light began to do two things:

expose our sin and show us a Jesus who stands ever ready to forgive.

N. T. Wright offers a helpful analogy about how God's grace comes into our lives. He compares it to waking up to an alarm clock:

Waking up offers one of the most basic pictures of what can happen when God takes a hand in someone's life. There are classic alarm-clock stories, Saul of Tarsus on the road to Damascus, blinded by a sudden light, stunned and speechless, discovered that the God he had worshipped had revealed himself in the crucified and risen Jesus of Nazareth. John Wesley found his heart becoming strangely warm and he never looked back. They and a few others are the famous ones, but there are millions more. And there are many stories, thought they don't hit the headlines in the same way, of the half-awake and half-asleep variety. Some people take months, years, maybe even decades, during which they aren't sure whether they're on the outside of Christian faith looking in, or on the inside looking around to see if it's real. As with ordinary waking up, there are many people who are somewhere in between. But the point is that there's such a thing as being asleep, and there's such a thing as being awake. And it's important to tell the difference, and to be sure you're awake by the time you have to be up and ready for action, whatever that action may be.[4]

The miracle isn't *how* you became a Christian, as wonderful as that may be. The miracle is that *you* are a Christian. To become a Christian is like the miracle of being born. This is one of the litmus tests to know whether or not you are genuinely a Christian. You think it's a miracle that you're a Christian. If God can save you, who can't He save? If your sins aren't too big for God to forgive, whose are?

My friend and fellow RUF minister Richie Sessions says it's like PE in your middle school days. If your school was like my school, we played a fair amount of basketball in PE. Typically, our teacher would pick two captains who would then pick teams. If you've ever been a part of this process, basketball or not, you know there are two kinds of picks: (1) The picks that will stack your team and (2) mercy picks. Mercy picks are the kids who will definitely double dribble and probably score on the wrong goal. If you're lucky, they might hustle, but even then, they'll probably foul a lot.

What Jesus is telling Nicodemus is that we're all mercy picks. There is no such thing as a Christian who isn't. And this is what Nicodemus can't bring himself to accept. He still thinks of himself as a first-round lottery pick. Like he can add something to Jesus's team. The only thing you bring to the table in your salvation is your need to be forgiven, your need to be made new.

Again, I relate so hard to Nicodemus. One of the first things I did when I became a Christian was get involved with a great youth group. The teaching was solid, and the worship was emotional in all the right ways. I wanted to be a leader in this youth group. If they made a TV show about that time of my life, it would have been called *So You Want to Be a Youth Group Hero?* Yes, please. I wanted the world to know Jesus. So naturally, I went to the closest Christian bookstore and looked into some of the most fashionable gear. It was pure providence that WWJD? bracelets had just been invented. I bought five, in different colors to match my different outfits. Navy was my everyday go-to. Next was hunter green. Throw a burgundy and black in the mix, and, of course, a khaki to make my Eddie Bauer khaki pants pop.

I wore my WWJD? bracelets with pride ... and a little bit of superiority. I was doing it. I was living like Jesus. The things so clearly near His heart were also near to mine: not cussing, not drinking, not smoking, not having sex (technically). Self-righteousness is a hell of a drug. I wore those bracelets until my life started coming off the rails in college, and in my deep shame, I found I couldn't bring myself to wrap them around my wrist anymore.

I wish there had been a different bracelet. I wish there had been a WJHD bracelet: What Jesus Has Done. What God would begin to teach me (and is still teaching me) is that the Gospel isn't good advice. It isn't a series of morals and principles with which to build a sin-free, God-approved life. The Gospel is instead good news, not about what you must do for God but about what He has done for you and me through the life, death, resurrection and ascension of His Son.

If you're reading this and want to design a WJHD bracelet, I'm fully ready to be your first customer.

The Results of Grace

Nicodemus is so close to the Kingdom … yet so far away. You can see it in the way he seems to think about Jesus. He sees Jesus as two things, mainly. First, Jesus is a great teacher. Nicodemus deeply believes that Jesus has a lot of great things to say. That when it comes to the way you should live life, Jesus has a lot of wisdom to offer, a ton of moral and spiritual insight.

Second, he also sees Him as a powerful miracle worker. It's undeniable that Jesus has done some pretty amazing and unheard-of things. He's healed the sick, the deaf, and the blind. He's turned water into wine. Nicodemus has heard accounts of these miracles and believes them, maybe even saw firsthand the undeniable results of some of them. But it's clear there's one thing he doesn't see in Jesus: He doesn't see Him as a savior. Because, if he's being honest, he doesn't really see any sin in his own life that he needs to be saved from.

This is why Jesus refers to that weird story about Moses and the serpent being lifted up in the desert. It's one of those Old Testament stories that we know exists but don't often talk about because it sounds a bit strange. In Numbers 21, the people of God have a reptile-infestation problem. Their camp is swarming with aggressive, poisonous snakes that are biting the people. When the people cry out for help, God tells Moses to make this bronze serpent and put it on a pole. Then, every time an Israelite is bitten, Moses would lift up the pole, and all they had to do was simply look at the serpent on the pole, and they would be healed.

Snakes in the Bible represent the curse of sin, and the bad news is we've all been bitten. So as he sits with Nicodemus, Jesus is saying, "I'm going to be like that bronze serpent held up in the wilderness. At the cross, I'm going to be cursed by God for your sin so that you might be blessed through My righteousness, Nicodemus. I'm going to become sin that you might become the righteousness of God. I'm going to be lifted up, and if you look to Me, believing in Me for salvation and healing, you'll be saved. Your problem, however, is that you don't see yourself as cursed. You think you already are the righteousness of God."

The way you know you've become a Christian, that you're growing as a Christian, is not that you're a good person. No. Instead, you begin to see more and more and more how cursed by sin you are, yet, at the same time, you also see more and more and more how Jesus became cursed for your sin that you might know the undeserved blessing of His love. The unmistakable sign of conversion isn't goodness but humility.[5]

It's like Brad Pitt in the film adaptation of *The Curious Case of Benjamin Button*. He's born an old man and strangely begins to age backwards. The older he grows, the more needy he becomes until he's a baby again, utterly dependent on the love and care of his parents. To grow as a Christian is to know your need for Jesus more and more, until you can say with John Newton on his death bed, "Although my memory's fading, I remember two things very clearly: I am a great sinner, and Christ is a great Savior."

The part I love about this story is the sequel. Nicodemus actually shows up twice in John's gospel. The first time is to secretly meet with Jesus. The second time is in John 19:39, when Nicodemus comes with Joseph of Arimathea to ask for Jesus's body so that they might give Him a proper burial. At some point, Nicodemus experienced this new birth Jesus was talking about. Why? Because the sin of his self-righteousness became so bitter that Jesus became sweet.

And if you do happen to make a WJHD bracelet, save me two. One to be buried *in*, and the other to be buried *with* so I can take it to my new friend Nicodemus. Scarlet red will do just fine.

CHAPTER 4

Even Disciples Get Jealous Sometimes

*"Therefore this joy of mine is now complete.
He must increase, but I must decrease."*

John 3:29–30 (ESV)

"As those who are chosen, blessed, broken, and given, we are called to live our lives with a deep inner joy and peace. It is the life of the Beloved, lived in a world constantly trying to convince us that the burden is on us to prove that we are worthy of being loved."

Henri Nouwen[1]

*"The most difficult lie I have ever contended with is this:
life is a story about me."*

Donald Miller[2]

Probably my very favorite SNL skit is the one where Will Ferrell and Ana Gasteyer play middle-aged parents, and the host that night, Sarah Michelle Gellar, plays their teenage daughter. It opens with the three of them quietly seated around the dinner table. The only sound you can hear is the clinking of their forks and knives on the porcelain plates. That is until they all start shouting over each other in explosive arguing, a chorus of angered voices ringing out, until one rings loudly above the other two as Will Ferrell suddenly shouts, "I am an important person! I drive a Dodge Stratus!"

A few years ago, I was re-watching the skit for the hundredth time when it suddenly dawned on me: we all have a Dodge Stratus. At the time, mine was ministry success. I was a young campus minister at Georgia Southern University in Statesboro, Georgia, and all I wanted was for my group to explode into the most impressive ministry on campus, numerically speaking. (Is that too much to ask? Jesus, give me humility, but not yet. Not yet.)

The sad reality is that you can make a Dodge Stratus out of almost anything (that actually may be true at the literal level too). Mine was ministry "success" at the time. But it has also been a girlfriend, an impressive Bible-reading streak, the approval of thousands of people on the internet, a Southern family heritage. In other words, a Dodge Stratus is anything we make an idol of, anything we look to to give us significance and value, other than the Lord Himself. We can worship at the feet of almost anything we feel makes us worthy of love, however ridiculous it might sound when we say (or scream) it out loud.

I have driven, and still drive, a Dodge Stratus, spiritually speaking. In fact, to wildly paraphrase John Calvin, my heart is a factory of Dodge Stratuses. (Dodge Strati? You get the point.) My heart, and your heart, can make an idol out of nearly anything, including good things.

Hey, Jealousy

When I look at John the Baptist's disciples arguing in John 3, I see so much of myself in them. If you don't remember the scene, they have experienced impressive ministry success by anyone's standards, even baptized Jesus Himself. Their brand has begun to get real recognition, their numbers have swollen, they are no doubt the talk of the town, plus they have a celebrity pastor in JTB (as the cool kids probably called him) that is unrivaled. Then this guy Jesus comes along and messes everything up as He starts His own public ministry. You can hear the jealousy flow from the hearts and drip from their lips when they say, "Look, [Jesus] is baptizing, and all are going to Him."

The person they are really jealous of is Jesus. Now, to be fair to them, they didn't know as much about Jesus as we do thousands of years later. They had been faithfully following their own rabbi, John the Baptist. Jesus has, in their minds, just emerged on the scene, and they're not quite sure what He is all about yet. But the irony is rich nonetheless. When we look with jealousy at the gifts of others or the success of others, isn't it ultimately a jealousy aimed at the One who gives the gifts and the success?

Their hearts are beginning to be exposed. Their Dodge Stratus is emerging. What did they really want? The same thing that most of us want: to matter, to be someone worthy of love and admiration. In their case, they had tasted it. And then this guy Jesus has begun to take it from them. In the words of Anne Lamott, "If you are what you do, and you fail, what then?" This is their "what then" moment. If ministry success is their identity, who will they be when it has faded from the spotlight into the shadows?

A short story by Fyodor Dostoevsky gets at the jealousy that runs amok in our hearts. In it, a man, weary with the world and himself, has decided to drink himself into a stupor and then kill himself in his apartment. But there's a problem. He's out of vodka. As he makes his way to the nearest liquor store, something strange happens. A little girl, no more than a few years old, waddles up to him and starts pulling at his trousers. He can't quite make out what she is saying, but he can tell that she is lost, separated from her parents. But his selfish despair runs deep that day, so he brushes her aside and makes his way back up to his apartment. As he is about to kill himself, he falls into a drunken stupor and has a strange dream. In it, he finds himself in a world untouched by sin. Everyone is only thinking about the good of their neighbor, only speaking words of encouragement and love. That is, until he arrives. And one by one, he begins to teach them how to lie, how to cheat, how to steal. The world darkens, begins to change, until, in the words of Dostoevsky, "[e]ach of them began to love himself better than anyone else. And indeed they could not do otherwise. Every one of them became so jealous of his own personality that he strove with might and main to belittle and humble it in others and therein he saw the whole purpose of his life."[3] In other words, everyone became so selfishly obsessed with themselves that they couldn't help but live in a constant state of jealousy.

The year I had an epiphany re-watching the SNL skit, my wife also asked me a question before bed one night that I'll never forget. Again, all I wanted in life was for our ministry to become something significant on campus, so that meant I was always trying to get impressive students involved. That year, I was sure I had struck gold. Two freshmen from Atlanta who were mega-gifted worship leaders—I'm talking discipled by Christy Nockels-type leaders—had arrived on campus and were both familiar with our ministry. I felt like a coach about to sign two five-stars that would change our program forever. Then something awful happened. They ended up with another ministry on campus. As I told my wife about it, looking for a partner in misery, she asked a heart-piercing question: "Sammy, do you think Jesus is disappointed with where they ended up?" It took everything in me not to say, "Yes!"

The question beneath her question was this: "Who do you want people to be enamored with? You—or Jesus?" If I'm being honest, can't it be both? Like love Jesus more, but also love me a lot.

You Down with JTB? Yeah, You Know Me

This is where JTB (still going with it) has a response of beautiful humility to his disciples. John is a weird dude for a lot of reasons. He is on the organic health food chain level before that is even a thing. He is a minimalist before there are documentaries and books about minimalism. Not that he is without flaws. He's not. He has his own moments where he's not so sure about Jesus, the most notable being when he's on the ancient version of Death Row and wonders if Jesus really is the Messiah for which they have hoped. "Is He bold enough?" John perhaps was thinking. But in this moment, John says something striking: "A person cannot receive even one thing unless it is given him from Heaven."

His logic is countercultural to a society that tells us to look deep within to find what we really need. Part of why we look with jealousy on others who have made it is, when we look at them and then look back at ourselves, we feel something must be lacking in us, wrong with us. This happens to me every day when I enter the brutal cycle that is my social media routine. I open Facebook and get disillusioned with a world that is as politically polarized as possible. Then I open Twitter and get disillusioned about the state of the world and my place in it. Then I open Instagram and get disillusioned about my own imperfect life. The whole time I'm either looking down on others or down on myself, and, in the words of C.S. Lewis, "A man cannot look up to heaven so long as he is busy looking down on everything else." Social media has the power to feed my pride while at the same time starving my humility. It has the power to keep me looking within and keep me from looking to Heaven and there seeing Christ, who is my life, seated at the right hand of the Father.

Years ago, NBA legends David Robinson and Michael Jordan were both inducted into the Hall of Fame on the same ballot. They both gave speeches at the ceremony, but their speeches were radically different. Michael Jordan, who is still one of the best, if not *the* best, NBA players of all time, proceeded to give a lengthy talk which was less a speech and more of a diatribe. He started with his first coach, then proceeded to critique every single coach he ever had, including Dean Smith, as well as a few teammates. He ended by critiquing his own children. It was truly one of the most self-serving speeches I've ever watched.

David Robinson's speech, on the other hand, was pure gratitude from beginning to end. He thanked his parents, every single coach he ever had, so many teammates, then finally his wife and children. He ended with the parable Jesus told about the ten lepers who were healed, but only one came back to express gratitude, which actually now that I think about it, may have been a little self-serving. Or a lot. But his speech was short and sweet and packed with gratitude.

A pastor reflecting on the difference in the two speeches pointed out that if you could have fast-forwarded them both, Jordan's would have sounded like, "Me. Me. Me. I. I. I," while Robinson's would have sounded like "Thank you. Thank you. Thank you." He then exhorted listeners to be like David, not like Mike. Be a person of deep gratitude, not deep pettiness.

It's hard being a person of deep gratitude when your heart is full of entitlement.

An entitled heart oozes with jealousy, not humility. Our hearts are broken in that way. Don't believe me? Just spend a few minutes on a social media platform of your choosing and see if Dostoevsky's words ring true: "Every one of them became so jealous of his own personality that he strove with might and main to belittle and humble it in others and therein he saw the whole purpose of his life."

How does one repent of jealousy and begin to live with gratitude? A couple hundred years ago, John Newton gave some helpful advice to a friend along that line: "I hope your soul prospers. I do not ask if you are always filled with sensible comfort—but do you find your spirit more bowed down to the feet and will of Jesus, so as to be willing to serve Him for the sake of serving Him, and to follow Him, as we say, through thick and thin; to be willing to be anything or nothing—so that He may be glorified? I could give you plenty of advice upon this head—but I am ashamed to do it, because I so poorly follow it myself! I want to live with Him by the day, to do all for Him, to receive all from Him, to possess all

69

in Him, to live all to Him, to make Him my hiding place and my resting place."4

He Must Increase

It was my wedding day, and I almost missed my bride. You know the moment I'm talking about. *The* moment. The one where the church doors are thrown open and everyone stands in unison and looks at the bride in all her beauty and glory—and I almost missed it. The problem was I had gone to the tanning bed for the first time in my life the night before (see my first book, *This Is Awkward*, for the full story), and my entire body was so badly burned that all I could think about was how much pain I was feeling. So when the time came to look to the opened doors, our pastor had to grunt at me to move into position so that I wouldn't miss the most important moment of the day: seeing my bride in all her beauty and glory.

The Christian life often feels like that. We get so consumed with ourselves—with what we're doing or how we're doing—that we are in danger of missing the whole point. The beauty and glory, not of the bride, but of our Bridegroom Jesus. The One who has come to love us out of our sins, to give Himself to us forever. Samuel Rutherford said it well about the church's love for Jesus, "The bride eyes not her beauty, but her dear bridegroom's face."

That's precisely the word JTB speaks to his disciples in the moment of their jealous fit. He gives them an illustration they won't soon forget. It's about a groom, a bride, and a best man, and he tells them that his role, and therefore their role, is to play the best man. In their day, the best man had quite the role to play, as he was in charge of making sure the wedding arrangements were taken care of and that everything was running smoothly. The role of the best man was to ensure the bride and the groom get hitched without a hitch. What would be weird is if the best man suddenly started making eyes at the bride, as if he were the point of the whole affair.

The illustration JTB gives is, of course, imperfect. Mainly because, in his case, he and his disciples are actually part of the Bride Jesus has come to take to Himself. JTB knows this, which is why, instead of being filled with jealousy at Jesus, he is filled with great joy. His whole ministry has been one of preparations, of making the arrangements, and now the Groom has come, and it has filled his heart with joy. But that joy is even more complete because he knows he is not just the best man, he is also part of the bride.

A few Christmases ago, when my kids were young enough to indulge my Christmas movie tastes, we sat down to watch a classic, *Rudolph the Red-Nosed Reindeer.* It had been years since I had seen it, and I was curious to see what their little eyes thought of claymation. As we were watching, we got to the scene where Rudolph (who, if you're somehow not familiar, doesn't exactly feel like much of a success), meets Clarissa, who upon meeting him, tells Rudolph that he's cute. These words knock Rudolph off his feet, and he begins prancing around, shouting out, "I'm cute! I'm cute! She thinks I'm cute!"

As we were watching, I started crying, and my kids began glancing at me from the side, their faces confused. What they didn't know is that, as I watching that scene, a question came to me, as if it dropped down from Heaven itself: "Sammy, what do you think I think of you?" I felt an overwhelming sense of the face of Jesus, full of affection, reminding me that I am one who the Lord delights in, and not because I'm delightful but because He loves me. If the Lord can speak through Balaam's ass, Rudolph is nothing.

I couldn't put it better than God already did through the prophet Isaiah. "You shall no more be termed Forsaken ... but you shall be called My Delight Is in Her ... for the Lord delights in you ... and as the bridegroom rejoices over the bride, so shall your God rejoice over you." As the bridegroom rejoices over the bride. That's what God thinks of you.

My favorite part of performing weddings isn't what you might think. It's not the part where the doors swing open and the father of the bride walks his beautiful daughter down the aisle. It's the part that happens while that is happening. My favorite part is to look at the groom's face as he watches the woman who has decided to marry him walk down the aisle. The joy on that face. The tears of wonder. The smile that says "I can't believe she is mine and I am hers." And for a moment in the face of the groom, I see the face of Jesus. It is a face so full of joy toward me, toward you, that I sometimes scarce can take it in.

CHAPTER 5

The Loneliness of Shame

*"We can only come to Jesus to drink if we are thirsty.
When we are full of ourselves, our power and certitudes, we think
we can do it on our own and fend for ourselves. We do not recognize
our need for new life. It is only when we present to Jesus our emptiness,
helplessness and broken hearts that he can fill us with the strength
of the Spirit and the touch of his love."*

Jean Vanier[1]

"Shame, boatloads of shame. Please make it stop. Please take it off."
The Avett Brothers[2]

"I believe no man was ever scolded out of his sins."
William Cowper[3]

We went too far. Again. I told myself we would never do it again, that instead we would pray together, read devotionals together, and stop doing the kinds of things we were doing. It all started innocently enough. Making out on the couch in my mom's living room. Our first kiss was halfway through *The Little Mermaid*. Full confession: I timed it so I would go for it during the "Kiss the Girl" scene, just like Ryan Gosling does.

But by the end of my senior year, things had started to go too far, and we both knew it but didn't know how to stop it. My lust was like a small campfire that, through carelessness, flamed into a forest fire, embering out into the woods until it began engulfing the life around it. How could I be the one doing this? I was a strong Christian leader, the kind who didn't miss quiet times, the kind who treated devotions like a devoted Crossfitter treats their workout of the day. My pride wouldn't let me confess my sins to a single soul. And my shame—well, it was crushing me. I was so covered in shame that all the showers in the world could never cleanse me from it.

Shame is a force in our lives. It tells us that we are what we have done. It whispers to us that no one will love us when they find out. Then shouts at us, the moment we get a little courage to be vulnerable, that we are not worthy of love. Unlikeable and unlovable. Shame tells us we are like the burnt fry at the bottom of the fast-food bag: Maybe someone is hungry enough to use us, but no one really wants us. Brene Brown puts it well:

Shame drives two big tapes—"never good enough"— and, if you can talk it out of that one, "who do you think you are?" The thing to understand about shame is, it's not guilt. Shame is a focus on self, guilt is a focus on behavior. Shame is "I am bad." Guilt is "I did something bad." She then asks her audience, "How many of you, if you did something that was hurtful to me, would be willing to say, "I'm sorry. I made a mistake"? ... Guilt: "I'm sorry. I made a mistake." Shame: "I'm sorry. I am a mistake."

A Thirsty Woman

Of the many challenges that come with raising teenagers, there are some perks too. One being the way you are forced, whether you like it or not, to keep up with the ever-changing lingo of youth culture. My son is particularly helpful in this regard. His obsession at the moment is Fortnite. (Lord, may this no longer be his obsession when this book finally comes out. Lord, hear our prayer!) I've learned that a "bot" is a kid who is basically bad at things, a fraud, a loser. I've learned that "you salty" is a way of saying you are perturbed, angry in a way that is noticeable to others. And my favorite one, at least for our purposes, is "he or she is thirsty," meaning they are desperate for attention and approval. That's the one I relate to most. I've been thirsty all my life, not just for attention and approval but ultimately for someone who can undo my shame, who can take away the loneliness it has caused.

We meet a woman in John 4 who is thirsty in that way. She comes alone to a well in the middle of the day because of the things her thirst has led her to do. When Jesus lovingly confronts the broken cisterns of her life, we learn that she has sought to quench her thirst through the attention and affection of men. She has apparently had five husbands already and has compromised with the latest one in some kind of common-law marriage situation. It's obvious that she isn't proud of these choices; otherwise, she wouldn't be at the well alone during the hottest part of the day. Her thirst has made her desperate. Her desperation has led her to dark places. Those dark places are a cause of great shame to her. And her shame itself is a great cause of loneliness. That's how shame goes. It makes you feel unlovable and therefore, very, very alone.

My first two years of college were some of the loneliest of my life. I could not escape my shame. I was too afraid to let go of a toxic relationship, and I was too afraid to let anyone in at the same time. How do you make friends when you are covered in shame? My first semester, I went home every single weekend, cutting off the possibility of new friendships, of getting involved. Then I convinced myself that, if I transferred somewhere else, I could escape my shame. So I tried. Made it a whole week at Clemson University before I came home, riddled with anxiety and depression, never to return. So I enrolled at the local branch of the University of South Carolina in my hometown for the rest of the semester and tried to carry the shame of living at home again. I felt as close to Matthew McConaughey in *Dazed and Confused* as possible, except there wasn't anything even a little bit cool about it. "I keep getting older, they stay the same age," isn't exactly a shame-free way to live. At least not for me.

By the time I eventually found my way back to the University of South Carolina, got back on my feet again, and even joined a fraternity the second semester my sophomore year, it was clear that the relationship I had clung to in my thirst was coming to an end. She was about to graduate high school and was exhausted from my all-consuming, hyper-controlling neediness. I didn't blame her. I was exhausted with myself. My last-ditch efforts were quietly refused, and I was finally left to pick up the pieces of wreckage shame had caused the last three years. I didn't get out of bed for a month straight, except to eat entire boxes of cereal. They tasted like shame.

Shame has the power to paralyze us. It cripples our ability to be what we could be, to be who God has made us to be. It tells us that no one could ever know what we did and still possibly want us or love us. It tells us that the only option left is to carry the weight alone for the rest of our lives—or worse, it tells us that life is over and there's no point in keeping up the pretense.

Shame doesn't just come with a script. It also comes with a filter. Listen to Ed Welch:

Someone says to you, "I love you." You hear ... nothing. Actually you hear something. You hear a little voice in your brain that says, "I'm worthless. You're only saying you love me because you think you have to." Somehow from the mouths of other people to your ear, all words of blessing and encouragement get tumbled upside down and backward and confirm your suspicions about yourself. You are an abject failure. Unloved. Unlovable. And everyone knows it ... This is your brain on shame.[4]

A Man Who Can Tell Us All that We Ever Did

Imagine being this woman for a moment. You come to this well for the thousandth time, but today, you're taken off guard. *A man is sitting there alone. Not just any man, a Jewish man. What is he doing in Samaria? Suspicious. And not just any Jewish man, a rabbi. Doubly suspicious. Where are his disciples? Obviously, he must be a little out of it, tired and thirsty and just sitting there. What is he waiting for?*

Then he strikes up a conversation, this man, this Jewish man, this rabbi! *He must be thirsty for something besides water. I've met men like this. He must want something from me. The kind of something that feels good for a moment, but then as soon as his thirst is quenched, he'll be on his way. But he seems different. He sees me. He seems to know me, wants to know me. Can I really trust him, though? I know what men are like, trust me.*

But he keeps offering me something I know my soul needs. The kind of water that wells don't hold that can quench the kind of thirst that water can't quench. He knows about my past, to my great shame, and yet my past, my shame, don't seem to deter him at all in his desire to know me and love me in a way that is beyond pure. Could this be the Messiah we keep hearing about? Could this be the One I've been waiting for?

This conversation with Jesus changes her so much that she leaves her empty water jar behind and goes into town and tells the men to come meet "a man who told me all I ever did." You can almost see the ears of these men perk up. They've probably wondered a bit themselves about the kinds of things she had done, to their shame. But apparently, they follow her back to Jesus, and as they meet the only One who can quench their thirst, a revival breaks out. Jesus takes the shame of one woman and turns it into the glory of an entire town. Our shame is no match for the grace of Jesus.

Come meet a man who told me all I ever did. And wants me. He knows me. He knows my past. He knows my present. He knows my shame. And He loves me. He wants to speak healing to my past and freedom to my shame. He wants to dry up the wells that have never been able to quench my thirst so that He alone may quench it in ways that make me forget about those old wells altogether. Who needs wells when you've started to drink from the Fountain of Life?

Malcolm Muggeridge, the successful British journalist who found Christ later in life, captured it well:

"I may, I suppose, regard myself as a relatively successful man. People occasionally stare at me in the streets. That's fame. I can fairly easily earn enough to qualify for admission to the higher slopes of the Internal Revenue Service. That's success. Furnished with money and a little fame, even the elderly, if they care to, may partake of trendy diversions. That's pleasure. It might happen once in a while that something I said or wrote was sufficiently heeded for me to persuade myself that I represented a serious impact on our time. That's fulfillment. Yet, I say to you—and beg you to believe me—multiply these tiny triumphs by millions, add them all together, and they are nothing—less than nothing, a positive impediment—measured against one drop of that living water Christ offers to the spiritually thirsty, irrespective of who or what they are."[5]

I Thirst

Shame has power because sin is real. Guilt connects to the part of us that knows we have sinned, but shame connects to the part of us that knows we are sinners. If it's true that we aren't sinners because we sin but sin because we are sinners, then shame is a powerful part of what it means to be human. That is, if we are sober about our own humanity, we can attempt to manage our guilt. Repent here. Get a bit more disciplined there. Read some practical books on conquering certain struggles, pray a bit more, start seeing a good counselor. These things can touch our guilt, but can they reach our shame? Who can touch our shame?

Not to mention the things that have been done to us that cause us great shame. The abuse we've experienced and the residue of shame we carry for the rest of our lives because of it. The shame that flows through our hearts through bullying, the names we've been called that stick in our brains like flies we can't seem to swat away. The shame of being unwanted by parents, spouses, and friends. We carry not only the shame of choices we made but also the shame of choices we did *not* make. The shame of what we've done, compounded by the shame of what's been done to us. Who can touch this shame?

As Jesus leaves Samaria and begins making His way to Jerusalem, His life gets touched more and more by shame. He's already experienced the shame of His mother's much-talked-about pregnancy with Him, surrounded by glares, followed by whispers, "Did you hear Joseph isn't the father?" He's also experienced the depth of poverty as a child, the kind where His parents could barely afford the cheapest possible sacrifices. He, though sinless, is no stranger to shame.

But His experience of shame is about to deepen. First, the shame of being deserted by His best friends, who selfishly no longer want to associate with a man under this much scrutiny. Then the shame of false accusations as He's brought to trial in a kangaroo court. The shame of injustice that follows. Though innocent, He's treated as the worst kind of criminal.

His shame intensifies even more as He's mishandled by the soldiers given charge of him. They strip Him, taking advantage of His naked body. They play games with the few of His belongings that are left. They play games with Him as they mock Him and call Him names. They beat Him beyond recognition. Then, when it doesn't seem like it can get any worse, the crowds join in, laughing at His naked, beaten body, condemning Him to death in a chorus of mocking disapproval.

As Jesus hangs on the cross, the cross that is itself the very symbol of shame, He gathers the strength to mutter a few last words. At one point, He is dying of thirst. Far more thirsty than the thirst He had experienced at the well that day as He met that woman in Samaria. With trembling lips, he stammers, "I thirst." The soldiers hear him, and in their cruelty hold up a stick of hyssop soaked in vinegar, the last liquid a thirsty man could ever want or need. Jesus dies in thirst.

The Son of God, in His humanity, got thirsty that day by the well. He was tired, weary from the sun beating on His back, and with aching feet and a parched throat sat down for a drink of water that day. The great I AM got thirsty. But on this day, the day of His death, he didn't simply get thirsty. He died in thirst. Why?

To understand the significance, you have to go back to the prophet Hosea, the one the Lord raised up to love a wayward woman. God tells Hosea to plead with the people of God in their adultery, saying to them, "Plead with your mother,

plead—for she is not my wife, and I am not her husband—
that she put away her whoring from her face, and her adultery
from between her breasts; lest I strip her naked and make her
as in the day she was born, and make her like a wilderness,
and make her like a parched land, and kill her with thirst."
The Lord is speaking in the passion of a spurned lover.

Yet Jesus dies in that thirst, as if He were the adulterous
spouse, not us. Jesus, the one who has never thirsted for anything other than doing the will of His Father, dies as if He were
the thirsty one, the one so desperate for attention and affection that He did things that brought great shame. Jesus is the
great shame bearer. "Bearing shame and scoffing rude, in our
place condemned he stood ... Hallelujah! What a Savior!"

Because Jesus died in thirst, in the place of the thirsty,
He can now invite those of us who are thirsty to come and
find Living Water in Him. Because Jesus died in shame,
He invites all those who have lived in shame to bring its
burden to Him. He still speaks through the prophet Isaiah
to every one of us who is tired of bearing the shame our thirst
has birthed. "Come, everyone who thirsts, come to the waters;
and he who has no money, come, buy and eat! Come, buy
wine and milk without money and without price. Why do you
spend your money for that which is not bread, and your labor
for that which does not satisfy? Listen diligently to me, and
eat what is good, and delight yourselves in rich food." This
is the voice of the One who can tell you all that you have ever
done in your thirst, yet who died in thirst so that you, with
the Samaritan woman, may never be thirsty again, forever.

Jesus is no stranger to your shame. Maybe you feel it is too much for Him to bear. Could He really tell you everything you've ever done and still delight to be your Savior? Could He really know your shame and still love you? Sinclair Ferguson puts it best. "In your shame, how could someone like you come to Jesus? Because he has come to your shame, to bring you to his joy." Why do you spend your labor for that which does not satisfy? Come to the waters and find your shame washed away and your thirsty heart filled with the living water of grace that Jesus alone can provide.

I wonder if C. S. Lewis had John 4 in mind when he wrote the scene between Aslan and Jill in *The Silver Chair*. Jill is dying of thirst and comes upon a flowing stream, but there's a problem. A giant, majestic Lion stands between her and the water for which she's so desperate. Lewis writes,

> "Are you not thirsty?" said the Lion.
> "I am dying of thirst," said Jill.
> "Then drink," said the Lion.
> "May I—could I—would you mind going away while I do?" said Jill.
> The Lion answered this only by a look and a very low growl. And as Jill gazed at its motionless bulk, she realized that she might as well have asked the whole mountain to move aside for her convenience.
> The delicious rippling noise of the stream was driving her nearly frantic.

"Will you promise not to—do anything to me, if I do come?" said Jill.

"I make no promise," said the Lion.

Jill was so thirsty now that, without noticing it, she had come a step nearer.

"Do you eat girls?" she said.

"I have swallowed up girls and boys, women and men, kings and emperors, cities and realms," said the Lion. It didn't say this as if it were boasting, nor as if it were sorry, nor as if it were angry. It just said it.

"I daren't come and drink," said Jill.

"Then you will die of thirst," said the Lion.

"Oh dear!" said Jill, coming another step nearer. "I suppose I must go and look for another stream then."

"There is no other stream," said the Lion.[6]

I've always loved the way that Ephraim the Syrian described the Samaritan woman. "At the beginning of the conversation he did not make himself known to her ... but first she caught sight of a thirsty man, then a Jew, then a rabbi, afterwards a prophet, last of all the Messiah. She tried to get the better of the thirsty man, she showed her dislike of the Jew, she heckled the rabbi, she was swept off her feet by the prophet, and finally she adored the Messiah."[7]

Jesus, no stranger to shame Himself, has come to undo our shame. He has come to repair all the damage it has done in our lives. Though our shame will resist Him, it is no match for the rescuing grace He means to bring.

CHAPTER 6

Do You Want to Be Whole?

"This man, closed up in pain, responds not from a place of faith but from a place of despair. He has no friends, no close family. Nobody cares for him. He is alone and abandoned to his dismal fate. In some ways he echoes the Samaritan woman who said, "I have no husband." I am alone; nobody loves me or wants me."

Jean Vanier[1]

"The great spiritual call of the Beloved Children of God is to pull their brokenness away from the shadow of the curse and put it under the light of the blessing. This is not as easy as it sounds. The powers of the darkness around us are strong, and our world finds it easier to manipulate self-rejecting people than self-accepting people."

Henri Nouwen[2]

"I think we need to get you to Charter Rivers." No ten words spoken to me before had ever struck fear into my heart like the ones my ears were now trying to take in. Charter Rivers is the mental hospital near where I grew up. The person speaking these words to me was my aunt. She was speaking them to me because, after the suicide threat I had made the night before, the next morning, I had driven my girlfriend and little sister at recklessly unsafe speeds on the way to meet my family for a beach trip. They were crying for me to slow down, begging for me to stop, but I felt my foot press down heavier on the gas. I wanted, needed, cellmates to join me in my prison of pain. I had become unhinged, madman-like in my mood swings.

The thing about depression is that it often comes in a package deal with repressed rage, so much so that some speculate that's what depression is—repressed anger. That it's anger that doesn't quite know how to work itself out, so instead it works its way in until it shuts down the person suffering with it and locks them up in a prison of apathy, a maze of despair. One moment, you are making plans to end your life, and the next, this rage surges through you toward the ones who love you. At least, that's how it was for me the summer after my junior year of college. It was the first time in my life that my brokenness was undeniable, yet I was terrified at the prospect of anyone or any place that might possibly help me find healing. Wholeness sounded harder than the brokenness I had slowly become accustomed to. Wholeness always seems harder than being comfortably broken.

It was clear to everyone around me, especially that day, that I was out of control. That was the feeling I hated, being out of control. So much of my anger and depression at the time was my response to feeling out of control. I wasn't in control of my dad suddenly leaving our family. I wasn't in control of the girlfriend who had suddenly broken up with me. I wasn't in control of the way I was feeling. I wasn't in control of my current girlfriend at the time, couldn't control her in a way that would ensure she wouldn't leave me. I was out of control because I was out of control. Couldn't control my life in a way that made it feel tame, unable to hurt me again. Marx said that religion is the opiate of the masses. I disagree. I think control is. The illusion that I could order my life in a way that put me "in control." To be the master of my fate, the captain of my ship. The only thing I felt like a master of was trying to control my life in a way that protected me from pain. It wasn't working. I was broken but did not want healing. Healing sounded painful. Plus, it sounded like something I wouldn't be in control of.

A Man Does Not Just Walk into a Pool

Several years ago, I had the privilege of leading a group of our students to work with a ministry on the south side of Chicago called Sunshine Gospel Ministries. One of our ministry opportunities for the week was to pack two lunches and take them downtown to share with the homeless. The idea was to actually share a meal with someone who was homeless. To ask their name and tell them yours. To ask about their story, gently and respectfully, and also tell them yours. As someone who normally waltzes past the homeless in a dance of fear and annoyance, this was a not-so-welcomed challenge.

The man we ate lunch with that day was named James. He hadn't been homeless for very long. Through a series of failed relationships, failed jobs, and failed attempts at finding another job, he had embraced a life of homelessness, resigned that no one in his family truly wanted to help him, resolved that this was what helping himself looked like. Forgetting the humanity of the homeless is one of the easiest things in the world to do. It's much easier to treat them as a strange subhuman species not to be trusted—much less embraced—like aliens in our midst.

This is part of what makes Jesus's encounter with the man by the pool in Bethesda so unusual. We are used to avoiding people like him at all costs. Drawing near is like looking into a mirror of what we easily could be with just a few bad breaks in life, a mirror image of how we all must look to God in our lost humanity, no matter how well we hide it before each other. But Jesus draws near, comes close, bringing the full weight of His compassion to bear on this man and his situation.

It is most definitely a situation, and hopeless at that. He has been badly crippled for thirty-eight years and is drowning in self-pity and despair, understandably so. He is physically crippled and also emotionally, relationally, and spiritually crippled; he is stuck in a hopelessness that is crushing him. No one will help him, he must think, because no one loves him, no one wants him, wants to know his name, much less his story. He is crippled by loneliness, too.

This is the man that Jesus meets. These are the people Jesus makes a beeline toward as soon as He comes to a new town. The ones who seem like hopeless cases. Steve Brown likes to say, "If you want to hang around Jesus, hang around pain. That's where Jesus likes to be." Jesus doesn't pass by this man in his pain, doesn't overlook him, look past him, or pretend not to see him. He sees him. He knows him. He cares about his pain. He is moved by his situation. He came not for those who are doing perfectly fine, thank you very much, but for those who feel the hopelessness of it all.

So much of this man's pain existed through no fault of his own. This man is a victim of the tragic forces of life, the kind that permanently damage. Yet, at the same time, this man, as we are about to see, has gotten used to the pain in such a way that he is doubly paralyzed. Paralyzed in his body, but also paralyzed in his soul's ability to face his suffering with anything close to resolve or hope. It is cruel to look at a victim and simply say, "Get on with it." But it is equally cruel not to offer the hope of getting on with it in a way where healing, if not physically, is emotionally impossible.

That is the sweet spot of despair. The spot between giving up and getting on with it. Jonathan Franzen described it well in *The Corrections*. He wrote, "The taste of self-inflicted suffering, of an evening trashed in spite, brought curious satisfactions. Other people stopped being real enough to carry blame for how you felt. Only you and your refusal remained. And like self-pity, or like the blood that filled your mouth when a tooth was pulled—the salty ferric juices that you swallowed and allowed yourself to savor—refusal had a flavor for which a taste could be acquired."[3]

A Good Question

"What do you do with your loneliness?" my counselor asked casually, as if he weren't surgically slicing my chest open and peering into my soul. A good question, a question like that, works its way through your best constructed walls of self-defense and draws the person you've been holding hostage out. The self you've been protecting, hiding, letting out only under the safest conditions. The one you've been hoping no one sees lest they call the authorities. You know, the real you.

The answer, of course, was not one I was proud of. *What do I do with my loneliness? How do I answer this with equal casualness in a crowded pizza shop? What have I done with my loneliness? I've taken it to porn. To food. To sleeping life away. To seeking for approval on Twitter. That's what I have done with my loneliness. I've taken it to anything or anyone but Jesus. Because can you really trust Jesus with your loneliness? Can He really turn the stale water of my loneliness into the wine of being fully known and fiercely loved? Can He really quench the thirst of the loneliness that has parched my soul?*

Jesus asks a similarly searching question of this man. "Do you want to be healed?" Do you want to be well? Do you want to be whole? It's like asking someone in the grave of depression "Do you want to feel better?" Or asking an addict "Would you like to be free from this thing that has consumed your life and tortured your soul?" The answer is a resounding "Yes! Of course, I want to be healed. Why would you ask a question like that?" Why does Jesus ask a question like that? Of a man like this?

Because, to use John's words, Jesus knows what is in the heart of man. He knows that it's a deep question. Not the kind meant to confuse or shame this man, as if Jesus were playing a game with him. But the kind meant to make him think, to make him wrestle with himself. Of course, the answer is "Yes, I want to be healed. Why else would I be sitting by this pool day after day?" And the answer is also "No. At least I feel some level of control, some measure of comfort with being the invalid who has sat by this supposedly miraculous pool for the last thirty-eight years." Our afflictions have a way of becoming our identity, the only way we know ourselves and, therefore, the only self we care to know. If we are not afflicted, who are we? If I am not the guy who struggles with depression, who am I? There is a comfort in familiar pain. There is fear in the unknown path of our healing.

In many ways, this man by the pool is like Naaman in 2 Kings 5. He was the commander of the king's army in Syria, but he was also a leper. He had no doubt learned to live with his leprosy—that is, until his army carried back a little girl from one of their raids in Israel. This little girl began working in Naaman's house with Naaman's wife and one day worked up the courage to tell his wife where her husband might find healing. If he would just go and speak with the preeminent prophet in Israel, Elisha could heal him of his painful condition.

So Naaman gathered his men and a ton of treasure and marched his way to the King of Israel, who pointed him to Elisha, who sent a messenger to tell Naaman what his cure would be. "Go and wash in the Jordan seven times, and your flesh shall be restored." Naaman's pride, already offended by the lack of regal welcome, could take no more. *Who is this messenger boy, and what kind of nasty river has the power to cure leprosy?* It was too much. Furious, he turned to walk away, but one of his servants stopped him. *Why not at least give it a try? Couldn't hurt anything but your pride.* So he did. And his flesh was restored. As clean as a newborn's.

When it comes to our healing, pride is our greatest enemy. Naaman's pride, when the prescription of his healing was given, swelled and said, "That boy! That river! Don't you know there are more important men and far better rivers? Don't you know who I am?" His pride almost cost him his healing. Same with us. Every time I suggest counseling to a student or to a friend and they push back, sure that they're not the type of person who really needs counseling, I love to say with a smile, "Why not try it? The only thing it can hurt is your pride, and that could be a wonderful thing."

One of my favorite scenes in C.S. Lewis's *Chronicles of Narnia* takes place in the *Voyage of the Dawn Treader*. In it, we meet Eustace, a boy so full of himself that he sucks all the air out of the room. Eustace is full of pride. We learn he is also full of greed, too. As the ship makes a stop on an island they've heard is full of treasure, Eustace is bent on finding it so that he might become rich. And he does. The only trick is there is a sleeping dragon guarding the mountain of treasure. Eustace decides he will carefully make his way past the dragon, but then something strange happens. He falls into a deep sleep, and when he wakes up, he doesn't recognize himself. His hands are now claws, his skin is now scales, and as he looks behind himself, he's grown a tail. To his horror, his dragonish heart has turned him into an actual dragon. He is desperate to go back to being a boy again. He flies through the sky, trying to get the attention of his cousins, trying to find someone, anyone, who can turn him into a boy again, until he finally comes face-to-face with Aslan. Aslan alone can un-dragon him. But he warns that it will be painful.

Eustace describes the scene. "The very first tear he made was so deep that I thought it had gone right into my heart. And when he began pulling the skin off, it hurt worse than anything I've ever felt ... Well, he peeled the beastly stuff right off—just as I thought I'd done myself the other three times ... And there I was as smooth and soft as a peeled switch and smaller than I had been."[4]

The Pride in Our Despair

The man by the pool is like Naaman because he has a desperate condition he hopes water can heal. But where Naaman's pride was the biggest obstacle to his own healing, despair is the greatest obstacle to the man by the pool's. Pride and despair might at first look like very different things. But in reality, they are often like two sides of the same coin. Where pride angrily says, "I deserve to be healed; it is my right!" despair wonders if healing is possible, "and if so, am I worthy of it?"

Jean Vanier shares the story of a man crushed by despair that made his way to their community, l'Arche in Chennai. His name was Sumasundra, a young man of twenty who had lived his days in a local psychiatric hospital after his mother abandoned him as a child. He was severely physically handicapped, with two deformed legs that made walking impossible. He had to drag himself through the streets. He would drag himself down to the local tea shop. His despair deepened when families would come visit his neighbors at the hospital, and he would search the room for his parents, only to be disappointed time and time again. He started dragging himself into the middle of the road, where cars had to swerve around him. A desperate cry for help, for death.

Vanier writes, "His despair came because he realized that his mother did not want him, could not accept him with his broken body. So he himself began to hate and reject his body. If people are not loved, they think it is because they are not loveable, that there is something evil and ugly in them."[5]

If pride says, "I'm not really as broken as you suggest," despair says, "I'm too broken for you to possibly love me." Pride and despair are both avenues of self-rejection and self-protection. Pride rejects the reality of my brokenness and, therefore, protects against either of us facing it. Despair rejects myself as broken beyond hope and, therefore, protects against anyone even trying to face our brokenness with us.

"Do you want to be healed?" Jesus asks this man. This man still thinks Jesus is offering His help to get him into the pool for his healing. He has no idea that the healing has come to him—not in a pool, but in a person.

The True and Better Pool

Just before Jesus starts His public ministry of preaching and healing, He does something strange. He goes to his cousin JTB (yep, still going with it) and asks to be baptized. John has been baptizing repentant sinners in the Jordan for months, and now the Lamb of God who takes away the sins of the world wants to be baptized along with them? It doesn't add up in John's mind. Jesus is the One who needs to baptize him, not the other way around! But Jesus insists, and so John baptizes Jesus in the Jordan River, the same one that Naaman reluctantly found healing in all those years before.

If baptism is a symbol of being washed and cleansed by the blood of Jesus, by the faith in that blood that is poured out to us by the Holy Spirit, why in the world would Jesus be baptized? We are baptized into Jesus's blood, but He was baptized into our sin. We take upon ourselves the cleansing righteousness of Jesus's pure and perfect life, but He took upon Himself the uncleanness of our unrighteousness, our impure and imperfect lives. The water that represented the sins of the people being washed away, those waters, full of our sins, are now being poured onto Jesus. Before we were washed by the cleansing blood of Jesus, He was washed in the shame-filled waters of our sins. So when the Father proclaims for all to hear that Jesus is His Son, in whom He is well pleased, He is saying it over us as well as the sinners Jesus has been baptized to reclaim.

This man expected his healing to come from someone, maybe Jesus, to help him into the pool that supposedly has healed others before. Instead, he finds his healing in the Man who was baptized into his sins, the One who has come to bring healing to hopeless cases. And Jesus does. By the same word with which He created the world, He now recreates the legs and life of this man.

This is where the story takes an unexpected turn. We would think it ends with this man running into the streets with those miraculously healed legs to tell everyone he can the good news about Jesus. He doesn't. The Jews find him walking, bed in hand, and they stop him. Doesn't he know he's breaking the Sabbath? He tells them what has happened, this miraculous healing, but he can't remember, either because he didn't catch Jesus's name, or, more likely, he doesn't want to be associated with this man the Pharisees have begun to hate. He has been physically healed, but his heart is still crippled by approval.

So Jesus finds him again and speaks a word of warning to him. Crippled legs are no match for a heart that has been crippled by sin. It's a warning against the Pharisees, who care more about catching people in sin, as they define it, than rejoicing in the healing of what the fall has caused. Jesus is saying be careful that the healing of your crippled legs leads to the healing of your greater problem: your crippled heart.

This time, the man uses those healed legs to run ... not to follow Jesus, but back to the Pharisees to snitch on Him. It's almost impossible to believe. Until you remember the last twenty-four hours of your own life and think of how easy it is to fear anything but the Lord, especially the disapproval of powerful men. His legs were healed. His heart still had a way to go.

One of my all-time favorite songs is by a band called The National. The song is called "England," and as best I can tell, it's a story about a time in the life of Matt Berninger (the lead singer) where he's gone through a painful breakup, of royally screwing up a relationship with someone he loved. The chorus is what gets me every time. I envision a house he's afraid to go home to, maybe because the memories are too strong there—or maybe it's because the rooms feel filled with nothing but loss. He can't face his own failure. He can't face his own loneliness.

And so the chorus goes, "Afraid of the house, stay the night with the sinners. Afraid of the house, stay the night with the sinners. Afraid of the house, cause they're desperate to entertain."[6] Any distraction from his loneliness, from his despair, is welcomed.

And I think about my own life. Do I want to be healed? Do I want to work through the anger I feel toward my own father for abandoning us? Do I want to work through the pain that he didn't love me enough to stay? Do I want to work through my own failures as a son, a friend, a husband, a father? Do I want to ask Jesus to touch the places of my life I've worked so hard to avoid, to reopen the wounds that have scabbed over with self-protection? Do I want to be healed? And I can almost hear my heart, the one still learning to walk in the ways of Jesus, I can hear it almost speak out of both sides of its mouth: Yes. And no.

CHAPTER 7

Can't You See?
Oh, Can't You See?
What Those Pharisees
Have Been Doing to Me

*"You search the Scriptures because you think that in them you have
eternal life; and it is they that bear witness about me, yet you refuse
to come to me that you may have life."*

Jesus, John 5:39–40 (ESV)

*"Jesus loves these Pharisees, and wants to break through their blindness
... But like so many of us, these Pharisees are stuck in their prejudices.
They do not want to be healed of their hardness of heart."*

Jean Vanier[1]

The internet can often feel like what the Tower of Babel must have felt like before the Lord put a gracious end to it. But occasionally, it gives us a gift, a treasure hidden in an often-toxic field. One of my very favorite such gifts is a short video series (think longish Vines) from a church in Raleigh, North Carolina, for a sermon series on "The Real Jesus." Essentially, they took footage from old Jesus movies and dubbed over them to make Jesus say the kinds of things we often (mistakenly) think He might say.[2]

One of the videos shows Jesus speaking with His disciples just before the Sermon on the Mount. Jesus goes to each disciple and critiques them, saying to Matthew, "I saw you smoking a cigarette last night." To John, "I saw you dancing a little too close to that girl last night." And then to Peter, "You were drinking wine last night. Not enough to get drunk but just enough to make Me angry."

I love that video so much because I think the kind of Jesus it portrays is the kind of Jesus the Pharisees craved. A Jesus who brings the hammer down on anyone not earning their keep. A Jesus who cares more about broken rules than broken people. A Jesus who has come to set the moral record straight, once and for all. A Jesus who came not to bear sin but to condemn sinners. A Jesus who came to discipline, not to die. So imagine their confusion when Jesus drew near to the very people they avoided. Imagine their confusion when He corrected them instead of praising them.

After I had just become a Christian, I went with my high school youth group on a mission trip to West Virginia. The house we stayed in had a couple of bedrooms upstairs for the guys and one bedroom downstairs for the girls, directly beneath one of the guys' bedrooms. That first night, an unfortunate event happened: the guys in the bedroom directly above the girls stayed up far too late and talked a little too loudly about the girls in ways that weren't exactly wholesome. And the girls heard everything.

At the same time, directly across the hall, a blossoming Pharisee (me) was leading a time of prayer in our room. My thought was "We're on a mission trip, so let's be as spiritual as possible" or something along those lines. So imagine my sheer delight when I heard the news over a very tense breakfast the next morning about what the guys in the other room had been up to. I couldn't wait to tell my youth leader.

It did not go as well as I had planned. Instead of him praising me for what an awesome young man of God I was, he gently rebuked me. Not with words, but with a face that was a mix of anger at my self-righteous glee and sadness that I would take joy in others' shame. He saw, in that moment, a young man who was turning the love of Jesus into a weapon with which to wound others. It's a face I hope never to forget because, in that moment, it was the face of Jesus.

External Appearance Over Internal Reality

Jesus's constant challenge to the Pharisees was the way they selfishly misinterpreted God's law. On the surface, they appeared to take God's law very seriously. They had a book of rules and regulations concerning the law bigger than your Southern Baptist grandmother's Bible. They weren't messing around. They wanted you to know that they took the law of God seriously, and if you didn't, they would never take *you* seriously. The problem was they were seriously mistaken in their understanding and application of God's law. It's not that they went too far. It's that they hadn't gone far enough.

A few Christmases ago, Santa (yep, we're those kind of Christians) brought my son a basketball goal for our driveway. Like most basketball goals, it is adjustable. So, because my son was nine at the time, we adjusted it down to about nine feet. Even though he is twelve now, his dad has been too lazy to take it up to the full ten feet that constitutes regulation size.

I say lazy. That's part of it. But the other part of it is ... do you know how good it feels to dunk on a twelve-year-old? It feels as good as an averagely tall thirty-eight-year-old with a definitely-a-dad bod suddenly becoming Lebron James. The sad reality, however, is that I've just left the goal adjusted for my advantage. Why? Because it makes me feel good. So good. Good enough to join Lebron with the Lakers, which might actually be realistic at this point.

The Pharisees were like that. They had adjusted the law of God down to something they could keep in a way that made them feel better than everyone else—as if they were religious versions of Lebron James amidst a sad host of terrible Lakers. They thought that because they had never had a physical affair, they weren't adulterers. They thought that because they had never killed a man, they weren't murderers. They thought that because they wouldn't carry their mats on the Sabbath, they were resting in God. They were, as Jesus tried to tell them, sadly mistaken. The God who looks upon the heart wasn't pleased with their outwardly apparent goodness. He wanted to go much further with them than that.

It's why Jesus told them the parable of the Pharisee and the tax collector. Here is this Pharisee who is very publicly praying in the market square (to be seen). The content of his prayer is a mix of telling God how good he's been and how bad he hasn't been. He prays not with contrition but with contempt. His prayer sounds less like praying and more like marketing. He is campaigning to be loved and accepted by God.

On the other hand, Jesus tells them, is a hated tax collector who is praying very differently, the kind of man no one is proud of knowing. And yet, as he prays, he pours out the sins and regrets of his heart, like a fire hydrant let open on a hot summer day. He is so focused on his own sin he barely notices the sins of others. "Lord, have mercy on me, a sinner." This isn't marketing. This is the kind of raw, yet hopeful, confession that Jesus says his Father loves. He's praying not to be seen but because he is a sinner. His hope isn't to prove himself faithful to God but to prove the promises of God are true even for him—that God is a God who loves to have mercy on sinners.

What Jesus is trying to tell these Pharisees is that a merciful God isn't an option when you don't believe you are a sinner.

No one has written about Pharisees with more devastating insight than Flannery O'Connor. In her short story "The Turkey," we meet Ruller, a young boy growing up in the country who longs, like all of us, to be loved and accepted as somebody important. Ruller is walking through the woods one day when he happens upon a strange sight: a turkey that's been shot without a hunter in sight. Ruller can see in his mind how the boys will celebrate him, so he throws the turkey onto his shoulders and heads back into town. As he's approaching, the boys start to gather around. This is it. This is his chance to be somebody. He can barely contain his grin as he turns around and asks them, "Y'all wanna see this turkey?" One of them responds, "Where did ya git that turkey?"

"I found it in the woods. I chased it dead," Ruller brags.

Then, much to Ruller's horror, one of the boys snatches the turkey from his shoulders and they all walk away. Ruller feels his aloneness. He feels the awful feeling about himself he felt before, but now it's worse, so he starts to run. O'Connor writes, "He ran faster and faster, and as he turned up the road to his house, his heart was running as fast as his legs and he was certain that Something Awful was tearing behind him with its arms rigid and its fingers ready to clutch."[3]

Ruller, like the Pharisees, mistakenly thought that to be loved, he must do something worthy of love. Unlike the tax collector in Jesus's parable, he hasn't learned yet that when you are already loved, all you must do is open your heart and spill out the parts of yourself that aren't yet walking in that great love. He hasn't yet learned that the Something Awful of the law is meant to lead him into the arms of Someone Better.

What Jesus has come to undo in these Pharisees is their own misconceptions about God Himself. They think *He* cares about the outward appearance of things, the keeping of rules, the record of achievement, the avoidance of sin. But Jesus has come to show them that God is far different than they thought. He isn't interested in what they have or haven't done for Him. He is interested in *them*—their stories, their pain, and their fears; in short, He is interested in their hearts.

Rules Over Repentance

Brennan Manning once wrote, "The temptation of the age is to look good without being good."[4] I'm not sure that's a temptation unique to our age, although social media has certainly made it easier. I think it's a temptation in every age. To wear the mask before God and others that makes me feel acceptable versus letting God and others see the real me, to quote Beyoncé, flaws and all. It's easy to be a Pharisee. It's easy for heartfelt, Spirit-led repentance to slowly transform into me thinking I'm a better Christian than you. It's easy for reverence to shift into self-righteousness. C.S. Lewis once warned a friend of this latter danger, saying, "It would be better not to be reverent at all than to have a reverence which denied the proximity."[5]

Before I was converted to Christ, I was converted to music. Specifically, the kind that was flowing from Seattle in the early '90s, later termed grunge. Music had become a refuge to me in the hurricane that was my parents' divorce. Pearl Jam, Nirvana, Smashing Pumpkins, Beastie Boys, and Sonic Youth were my guides now. Their sadness and angst got me and got me through some hard years. I now had close to three hundred CDs, and they were my prized collection. And then I met Jesus. After a year of growing in my love for Him, I felt like it was time to let go of that CD collection, to repent of looking to music as a kind of savior instead of Jesus.

Now, from this side of things, I wish very much an angel of the Lord had stayed my hand as it plopped those three hundred CDs on the counter at CD Switch, but the Lord works in mysterious ways, and I sold those CDs and got about $150 in return. I decided to make a return on the investment and poured that $150 into Christian music (thankfully Tooth and Nail had come on the scene). I can still vividly picture the poster in the CD section of the local Christian bookstore that compared your favorite secular bands to current Christian ones. "If you like Pearl Jam, then check out The Prayer Chain" and "If you like Green Day, check out MxPx." It probably should have read, "If you like good music, then Christian music will deeply disappoint you."

For the next four years of my Christian life, I pretty much held to a simple rule: serious Christians DO NOT listen to secular music. Sure, I flirted with a little Our Lady Peace my senior year of high school. Yes, I got a little crazy with some Creed (technically they were kind of Christian). And I'll never forget asking my best friend if I could borrow the latest Sonic Youth CD (*Washing Machine*) for a week, listening to it like my ears were dying of thirst, then guilty returning it to him that next week like it was an empty bag of cocaine.

I'll also never forget the moment I realized how dumb this self-righteous rule was. It was my freshman year of college, and I had just met another Christian on campus, which felt like a small miracle, and the first thing out of my mouth as a follower of Jesus was "Yeah, I only listen to Christian music"—and when I say "first thing," I mean within the first ten minutes of meeting this brother. It's like Jesus said, "The world will know you are My disciples by the way you avoid all secular music like the plague."

My problem was that I had turned a genuine, even if slightly misguided, moment of repentance into some kind of golden rule by which *all* Christians should have to live. We call that self-righteousness. It is a spiritual disease that slowly kills the hearts of those who love Jesus, and we are all carriers. It is a silent killer. It looks like righteousness, but behind the curtain is the pride that says, "Look at how faithful I am!" instead of the genuine righteousness that says, "Look at how faithful God is."

And we can do it with almost anything. Mine was Christian music. But it was also cussing, smoking, drinking, having sex-sex (that's the one that eventually got me). I suppose now it's not being on certain social media platforms, only eating certain kinds of food, or religiously working out. The point is that self-righteousness is a shape-shifter, taking the appearance of good things while hiding the proud motivations that are its essence. I guess that's a long way of saying self-righteousness is like Mystique from X-Men—before she repents.

All it takes to be a Pharisee is to lose sight of the hourly repentance that is the flip side of faith and to focus instead on a set of rules that are relatively easy to keep. There are plenty of ways to cut others down without ever saying a cuss word. And not smoking is a whole lot easier than repenting of the ways you've failed to love your neighbor. It would be far better, and you would be closer to the Kingdom, if you split a pack of Parliaments with your neighbor instead.

A Pharisee Toward Pharisees

A friend was recently telling me about one of the hardest church experiences he had ever gone through. His family had recently joined a new church and didn't exactly feel like they were fitting in. Like bringing a knife to a gunfight—except in his case the knife would be casual clothes and less obedient children.

This one particular Sunday, his wife and oldest daughter were helping watch the nursery, which meant he had the hard job of watching his other three kids by himself through the service. *Cool. Just bring plenty of markers and paper and we'll make it*, he thought. *Just make it through the service without killing one of your children*, he thought.

That was until he had a horrible onset of potential diarrhea. The kind where you're not sure you can actually make it to the restroom on time. What was he supposed to do? His body decided for him, and his kids were left for the next ten minutes to police themselves in the pew. When he got back, it was Lord of the Flies. Volume levels were up. A case of the giggles ran through all three kids like firecrackers on the Fourth of July. He was that mix of angrembarassed that only parents trying to keep their kids in check in public know.

Then he reached a breaking point. The whole time, a very well-groomed dad, with his very well-behaved daughters, who had been sitting a few rows in front of them, had been looking back at them. You know the kind of look. The one that says, "How can you even call yourself a Christian letting your kids look and act like that?" The look of complete and utter disgust. The Very Well-Groomed Dad had already given about five of them, and my friend, we'll call him the Very Angrembarrassed Dad, had caught all five, so by the sixth one, he decided to stare back, as if to say, "Fellow dad, please give me the grace of knowing that I'm trying my best." It was, I imagine, a lightsaber battle of looks. The Very Angrembarrassed Dad lost. Like Anakin Skywalker by the banks of that lava, he was then fully prepared to go Darth Vader on Very Well-Groomed Dad.

Let me just say that the last thing a parent struggling with their kids needs is another parent's judgment. They have already judged themselves, and they are desperate for kindness, for mercy, and for help when it's appropriate. The last thing they need is for you to stare at them in a way that makes them feel more burdened and more alone. That's the burden that Jesus rebuked the Pharisees for placing on their disciples.

The kind that was already back-breaking to carry, but then even more crushing when the ones judging them would not lift a finger to help them carry it.

It's easy for me to listen to my friend and hate the Very Well-Groomed Dad. Why did he feel the need to keep looking at my friend and his kids? What did he think his angry stares would accomplish? Was he aware that my friend saw every one of them? Felt them, too?

But then my friend had a sequel to the story. He was sitting in a crowded restaurant, enjoying a meal with a good friend, when all of a sudden, the Very Well-Groomed Dad walked in with his family. The hostess seated them in the booth right behind him and his friend. He told me that, instead of greeting the Very Well-Groomed Dad with kindness, he chose instead to slink out the side door with a heart full of hatred. That's when it dawned on him: If Jesus loves Pharisees, who is he to hate them? Jesus wasn't a Pharisee toward Pharisees but was full of meekness and kindness toward the very people who hated everything those words represent. Yes, He confronted them and challenged them. Yes, their self-righteousness made Him righteously angry. But He always had the heart of a mother hen, longing to gather them under His wings.

A God Who Loves Pharisees Too

Frederick Backman's *A Man Called Ove* is the story of an old curmudgeon being loved back to kindness by a community of misfits he, at first, tries to escape and avoid with all his might.

Ove is described as a man who "saw the world in black and white" and "went through life with his hands in his pockets."[6] But his neighbors, especially a young Muslim immigrant mother, Parvaneh, sees through his hard exterior and finds his grumpy disdain for nearly everything amusing. So she decides she will push through all his attempts to isolate himself in his "rightness" while avoiding all the stupid people he can't help but judge for their "wrongness." It is the story of a cold, hard man being loved back from the dead into a life of kindness and joy. Parvaneh is a small picture of what it means to love Pharisees.

If the Pharisees were challenged by Jesus's love for sinners, then Pharisees toward Pharisees need to be challenged by Jesus's love for Pharisees. Jesus didn't end His parable of the two lost sons in Luke 15 with the younger brother going to his father to complain about how his older brother didn't get grace. He ended it with the father stepping outside the party to plead with the older brother to come inside. The younger brother, as he was really getting grace, would be right behind him. Inviting him to humble himself and come drink the good wine of being loved by the Father, just enough to be drunk on His love.

Because Jesus loves sinners, He loves Pharisees too. He loved Nicodemus, and soon enough, Jesus became so precious to Nicodemus that he went, not in the dark of night, but with Joseph before the authorities to dignify Jesus's crucified body. He loved Paul, and soon enough, Paul became not a Pharisee of Pharisees but a humble champion of the grace of God that is greater than all our sin. He loved Peter, through Paul, who confronted Peter in his racism and classism, and soon enough, Peter starts encouraging the church "to clothe yourselves, all of you, with humility toward one another, for God opposes the proud but gives grace to the humble."

It was, no doubt, the Pharisees who killed Jesus. Those who couldn't stand the love and kindness and meekness and weakness that Jesus lived and preached. Those who were jealous of His success. Those who hated Him for how He opposed their ways and traditions.

But there is no doubt that Jesus died for Pharisees. That He stands by the door, pleading with them to come in, to leave their empty performances and achievements behind and to come and feast on His grace with joy. That He invites them to trade in their marching for dancing, their rules for repentance, and their reputations for being loved infinitely more than they have yet imagined. That He invites them to learn from Him how to cry, how to laugh, how to love, and, yes, even how to be angry without sin.

In the Kingdom of God, every day is Hug a Pharisee Day. Hug them until the kindness of God leads them to repentance. Then hug them some more. There is a strong chance you needed that same hug, and still do.

CHAPTER 8

A Love Stronger Than Death

"Jesus wept."
John 11:35 (ESV)

"We sing 'Amazing love, how can it be, that thou, my God wouldst die for me.' But we can also sing, 'Amazing love, how can it be, that thou, my God, wouldst cry with me.'"
Frederick Dale Bruner[1]

"No one else, however well disposed, is ever in a position to be with us so completely that we feel ourselves to be understood and loved without limit. We humans remain too self-centered to be able to forget ourselves fully for the other person's sake. But Jesus does give himself fully, he holds nothing back for himself, he wants to be with us in so total a fashion that we can never again feel alone."
Henri Nouwen[2]

You haven't lived until you've very publicly ugly-cried in a Starbucks. It's happened to me twice. The second time I will get to later in this chapter, but the first time snuck up on me, like a ninja that came not to kill me but to hug me in a very *Good Will Hunting* way, telling me, "It's not your fault." It was a conversation with my then-intern, and now great friend, that did it. We were talking about ministry, and I was complaining in the very specific and painful way depressed people are prone to do. I was complaining about low numbers and a lack of what I deemed proper enthusiasm in the response to my sermons (anything less than a standing ovation was disappointing, even though I've never gotten one). She listened. Listened some more. Then, with the gentleness of Jesus, she asked a soul-searching question: "Sammy, I know you believe that Jesus loves you. But do you believe that he actually *likes* you?"

Do you believe that Jesus doesn't just love you but actually enjoys you? Looks forward to time with you? Misses you when you withdraw from Him? Has great affection and warmth for you? Do you believe that Jesus actually *likes* you?

To be honest, it's hard for me. But the story that unfolds in John 11, where Jesus grieves with his great friends, Martha and Mary, over the death of their brother and his beloved friend, Lazarus, helps me because Jesus shows, with words and actions, that He more than loves Mary, Martha, and Lazarus. That He likes them so much, He has spent a significant amount of time with them. He has enjoyed Martha's home-cooked meals. He has lounged with Mary at His feet. He has spent late nights in Lazarus's house, no doubt laughing and praying and listening and counseling with him. This brother and these sisters are dear to Jesus.

Which is why one of the most confounding verses in all of Scripture is chapter 11:6, "So, when he heard that Lazarus was ill, he stayed two days longer in the place where he was." Why doesn't it say, "So when He heard that Lazarus was ill, He rushed with His disciples to the place where he was"? If Jesus more than loves Mary, Martha, and Lazarus, then what is He thinking?

Waiting on the Lord

A few years ago, Jon Acuff wrote a blog post called, "Good Sex, Flat Abs, and Jesus." In it, he shares a funny thing that happened to him. He was in the book section of a Walmart and noticed something strange: the inspirational lines on the front covers of men's and women's lifestyle magazines were eerily similar to the lines on the back covers of the Christian inspirational books across from them. So he decided to give a little quiz to see if readers could guess which one certain lines were from. For example, "Uncover the proven process that will lead to a life of success and total fulfillment." Front cover of a lifestyle magazine or back cover of a Christian book?

Reflecting on this disturbing revelation, he concluded, "Do I ever go to God with a laundry list of 'better' demands? Give me a better marriage, a better ministry, a better life, a better job, a better everything? Do I chase the blessings of God sometimes more than His presence? Do I ever treat God like a really good self-help guru that is there to meet my needs? Yes, yes I do. But I don't want God to simply be a new vehicle for the things I want. I want God to be what I want. I want Him to be enough."

It seems that some of the most important work Jesus does in our lives is to disappoint us. I don't mean that in the sense that He isn't there for us. The reality of John 11 is that Jesus is coming to be with His friends, and He is coming to do something about their pain. But they don't know that at the time. In their pain, they are asking themselves, asking each other, "Where is Jesus? Why isn't He here yet? Does He even really care about us?" It's reminiscent of Psalm 88: "O Lord, why do you cast my soul away? Why do you hide your face from me?" Or in the words of Kendrick Lamar, "Is there anyone praying for me?"

Jesus loves His friends enough to disappoint them—not because He doesn't care but precisely because He cares so much for them. He disappoints them so that their hope will not be in what He can *do* for them but in who He *is* to them. Jesus refuses to simply be a vehicle for the things we want. He loves us enough to disappoint us so that our hope would not be in what we can get from Him but in the way He has given Himself to us and for us.

Around the same time I ugly-cried in Starbucks (the first time), I had another conversation that will always stand out to me. It was a phone conversation (Millennials and Gen Z-ers, look away) with a friend right after a Wednesday night large group ministry meeting. We both had our large groups on the same night, and would often call to check in on each other. The loneliest hours in ministry are the ones right after the meeting or service where you are your own worst Simon Cowell, critiquing yourself into a fetal position. That particular night stood out to me because half of my group forgot to show up. At least that's what I thought … until a student later informed me that a ton of students weren't there because they had gone to an Owl City/John Mayer concert in Atlanta instead. (I still tear up when I hear "Fireflies.")

I was sharing all of this with my friend who was the Reformed University Fellowship campus minister at the Savannah College of Art and Design in Georgia at the time. He had also had a disappointing turnout that night, so we were commiserating. Then he said, "Sammy, I think Jesus loves me too much to give me a big large group right now." The truth of what he said was like a grenade that had just been lobbed into my soul. Jesus loves me too much to fill in the blank with whatever current idol I'm worshipping at the moment. For me, and for him, it was impressive ministry success at the moment. But it has been all kinds of other things throughout my life, from a girlfriend to a bestselling book. *Jesus, if You love me, give me what I want (or at least what I think that I want), even if it won't be good for me,* and Jesus loves you and me enough to say, "No. I love you too much for that."

I think about one of the most underrated John Newton hymns, far less popular than "Amazing Grace." It's called "I Asked the Lord," and in it, Newton tells a familiar story. It's about a zealous young Christian praying that the Lord would make him even more zealous, make him feel yet more of God's goodness and presence. That's the first stanza. The next seven or eight are all about how the Lord seemed to do just the opposite of his request. Instead of life getting easier, it got harder. Much harder. Instead of life getting simpler, it got more and more confusing. The hymn ends with a stunning realization:

Instead of this he made me feel
the hidden evils within.
Crossed all my fair designs and schemes,
that thou mayst seek thy all in me.

The hard yet freeing truth is that if Jesus never makes us wait, we will never learn to wait on Him. If He only existed to be a vehicle for the things we want, the things we want would become our god, and there is no other god who can love us like Jesus. He even knows how to take the pain of the worst losses we've experienced and turn them into our healing.

Great Shining Tears

The second time I ugly-cried in a Starbucks happened a few years ago. I was with a mentor, and we were processing how my dad had left our family when I was twelve years old because of a crack cocaine addiction that had taken his life hostage. We were talking about how the pain of that abandonment had shaped so much of my life, and as we were talking, my mentor lovingly said, "If you are ever going to find healing, the adult you is going to have to go back to the twelve-year-old you, hold his hand, look him in the eye, and tell him, 'Sammy, Dad's not coming home.'" Tears shot horizontally from my eyes, which actually may have helped the coffee taste a little less burnt, now that I think of it.

My whole life, I have longed for a rescuer. Someone who doesn't just come to tell me things are going to be OK, but someone who comes and makes them OK. In my head, I know this is Jesus, but in my heart, anyone else will do. Besides, how do you trust a God who lets dads leave twelve-year-old little boys to fend for themselves? Sometimes, the painful things Jesus allows to happen in our lives are so much that the thought of trusting Him ever again seems not just hard, but unthinkable. Does Jesus care about our pain? Does He feel it the way we do?

Back to Starbucks. My mentor has spoken this painful and powerful word to me, I'm ugly-crying (again) in a Starbucks, and I suddenly hear that still, small voice that speaks in and through our pain, and it's as if the Lord says to me, "Yes. We do need to go back to twelve-year-old Sammy and tell him Dad's not coming home. But I want to be there too. And I want to weep with you."

The greatest Christian theology can be condensed into two words: Jesus wept. The Son of God, who made the world in glory, along with the Father and the Spirit, is the same Son of God who wept over its brokenness. The God who made Martha and Mary and Lazarus, who knit them together in their mother's womb, who knew them before they were even born, is the same God who begins to bear their sorrows with great shouts and loud cries. I could never trust a God who had no tears. Jesus wept.

It would be better to say that Jesus burst into tears. Jean Vanier writes, "It is difficult to translate the Greek verbs [in John 11]; I have translated them as 'shuddered' and 'agitated.' … Jesus shudders, he is in anguish, he gives out a cry of pain."[3] His tears did not go gently into that good night; they raged, raged, against the dying of the light. These weren't sentimental tears, as if Jesus had just been polishing off a bottle of wine as He listened to the latest Bon Iver album. And they aren't regretful tears, as if Jesus, like Oskar Schindler, was bemoaning what could have been, how much more he could have done.

The tears of Jesus were angry tears, for death is a great enemy of His people. The tears of Jesus are loving tears, for He cares deeply for His friends and feels deeply their pain. The tears of Jesus are sacrificial tears, for He knows the tomb He is about to approach is strikingly similar to the tomb in which He will be laid. Jesus has come to die in love that His love will prevail over death itself. Jesus has come to give Himself, even to a cruel and unjust death, that His friends might never truly die. These are the tears Jesus is crying. These are the tears that speak to the horrors of the pain, the loss, the injustice, and the crushing loneliness we carry like burdens on our shoulders and wounds in our bodies. Someone isn't just praying for us. Someone is crying with us.

There's a scene in C.S. Lewis's *The Magician's Nephew* where Aslan finally shows up at Digory's mother's deathbed. It's all Digory has wanted, what he has been asking Aslan for throughout the entire story. He just wants Aslan to stop his mother from dying. To take the pain of death away. Lewis writes, " 'But please, please—won't you—can't you give me something that will cure Mother?' Up till then [Digory] had been looking at the Lion's great feet and the huge claws on them; now, in his despair, he looked up at its face. What he saw surprised him as much as anything in his whole life. For the tawny face was bent down near his own and (wonder of wonders) great shining tears stood in the Lion's eyes. They were such big, bright tears compared with Digory's own that for a moment he felt as if the Lion must really be sorrier about his Mother than he was himself."[4]

Dad's not coming home. Mom's going to die. Lazarus is dead. Each of these moments brings great tears of greater sadness and loud cries, even, if we let ourselves feel them. But just as there are wounds that speak to our wounds, there are tears that speak to our tears. The great shining tears of Jesus, who must really be sorrier about the suffering of this world than we are ourselves. And He has come, not just to weep with us in sadness. He has also come to make the sad things come untrue.

Wake Up, Wake Up, Wake Up. It's the First of the Month

I've been to thirteen funerals in my life so far, and I'm sure there are more that I'm not remembering. Some of those funerals have been the funerals of loved ones, and they've left a gaping hole in my life. Others have been funerals of loved ones of those I love, and I could feel that same hole ripped open in their lives. One funeral in particular stands out to me. It was actually a visitation. The dad of one of my best friends in college had died suddenly, an unexpected heart attack. My wife's own father had died the year before of multiple myeloma, and so even though I hadn't seen my friend in years, I had learned firsthand how much it means when old friends show up to grieve with you as best they can. So I got into the car and drove to the visitation.

As I made my way in the receiving line, I kept thinking about what I would say to my friend. I hadn't seen him in a long time, and the awkwardness of speaking to his pain from that distance felt hollow. How can we who haven't kept in touch suddenly reach out to touch the pain of old friends? Then I saw my friend. No words were spoken before he burst into tears, which made me burst into tears, and we simply hugged for several minutes. Pain is more bearable when shared.

That's how it goes with us. We go the visitation, to the funeral, to the grave, and then we cry. Or try to cry, try to let ourselves access and admit the pain we otherwise do our best to keep at bay. Jesus does the opposite. In the words of Tim

Keller, "Jesus weeps, then goes to the grave."[5] He has something to say to it.

The miracles of Jesus have never impacted me the way I want them to. Maybe it's because I wasn't there, and so the shock of them is lost on my imagination. Or maybe it's because I've gotten so used to them, know the stories so well, that they somehow feel less real, less historically amazing and confounding. Or maybe it's because I'm Presbyterian and am generally suspicious of words like "miracle" and "experience" and "feelings." It's not that I don't believe that Jesus raised Lazarus from the dead. It's that I'm left wondering what it has to do with me.

It wasn't until I started to understand that the miracles of Jesus were more than great displays of His unique identity, mission, and power that I connected with them more. This miracle isn't less than that, but it is so much more. It is a foretaste, a sample, of what Jesus has come to do, or better put, what He has come to undo. In this case, He raises Lazarus from the dead to give us a taste of how exactly He will make the sad things come untrue. In Lazarus's resurrection, Jesus gives us a foretaste of the very real promises of His own resurrection. Christ raising Lazarus from the dead is a small picture of what it means that we have been raised with Him from the dead as well.

My family is the kind of family that celebrates everything with food and drink. My wife, much to her horror, has learned that any trip we take, whether it's to Washington, DC, or the Grand Canyon, all I'm thinking about the whole time is what we will eat and drink next. You can have Mt. Rushmore. Give me Jerry's Donuts instead. Sometimes, when we can afford it (or if someone else is paying) there's nothing better than ordering a reasonably overpriced bottle of wine to enjoy with dinner.

The moment I always low-key dread is the moment after ordering the bottle of wine when the waiter brings it over, uncorks it with ease, and pours a small amount in my glass for me to taste. So I swirl it, let my nose hover over the glass for what I hope is an acceptable amount of time, then taste it—I suppose to make sure that it hasn't spoiled. I'm at my fakest when sampling wine. The whole ordeal is simply meant to ensure that I've enjoyed what I've just tasted because there is a whole bottle of that to come. I've always wanted to muster up the courage to send a bottle back in the kind of power move that surely only Enneagram Eights have enjoyed, but alas, I am far too driven by approval, even from a random waiter, to ever do that. (A boy can dream.)

This is what Jesus is doing in Lazarus's resurrection: He is giving us a taste of the resurrection feast to come. He is showing us that His tears are not in vain because His love is stronger than death. Not even death itself can separate us from the love of Jesus, who died the death that we deserve, that He might bring us into a resurrected life that we could never earn. A life of feasting with Him eternally, where the wine never runs out because the presence of Jesus abounds.

Today is my birthday, and instead of being at home with friends and family, I'm at a monastery working on this book.

I've never celebrated a birthday by myself before, and I have to say, as an introvert, it's incredible. Sometimes the best gift is no people. But as a human being, I have to admit I'm a little sad. We celebrated early, and there were gifts, and I ate a good working on a definitely-a-dad-bod amount of caramel cake. But today, there are no presents to open, and it's a little sad and a little weird.

That's why I love the image John leaves us with in this story. It's of Lazarus, fresh from the tomb, wrapped head to toe in grave clothes. Jesus says, "Unwrap him." Whether it's our birthday or not, this is the gift every Christian needs. It's the gift of resurrection grace that says Jesus will make all the bad things come untrue, even the ones you've just gone through. Lazarus's resurrection is a foretaste, but Jesus's resurrection is a promise. A promise to all of those who have ever wept bitter tears through the night, that joy, laughter even, will be there in the morning. That He sheds tears with us now but then will wipe our tears away forever.

CHAPTER 9

Loved to the End

*"Having loved his own who were in the world,
he loved them to the end."*

John 13:1 (ESV)

*"In that very room where they had every reason to know that something
fateful and tragic was about to happen to the leader they swore they
loved, it is their own fate they are worried about as they set about
jockeying for position. '[L]et the greatest among you become as the
youngest, and the leader as one who serves,' Jesus says, and you can hear
the weariness in his voice as he says it, wondering if it can be possible
after all he has tried to show them both with his words and with his life
that they have still missed the whole point on everything."*

Frederick Buechner[1]

The Hallmark card read, "I love you." I was seventeen; she was fifteen. We were parked in my mom's 1992 white Toyota Camry, which she had let me borrow for what was our second real date. The date had started at the only real chain restaurant in my small Southern hometown, an Applebees, which could explain a whole lot of my depression. We went to the same high school but had officially met at youth group. I was a rising senior; she was a rising sophomore. It was safe to say that I was smitten. It was also safe to say that, as I handed her this card on our second real date, the card professing my love for her, she was no doubt terrified. Can you really love someone after two dates? Can you really love someone when you're seventeen? Or fifteen? These are the kinds of situations for which we would actually use time machines. Stopping Hitler. Check. Stopping myself from an embarrassing profession of "love." Double check. Maybe I was in love. Then again, maybe it was the delicious Applebee's chicken tender basket with extra honey mustard.

Whether my professed love was real or not, my desire to be loved was very real. Palpable even. The Beatles famously sang, "All we need is love," but in reality, what we need is to *be* loved. It's been said that love makes people do all kinds of crazy things, but it's probably more psychologically correct to say the need to be loved is what drives our own particular version of crazy. I was desperate for love, and along came a girl that might could meet that need. ("All we need is to be loved, doo doo doo da doo." Not quite as catchy.)

Robert Penn Warren described the sensation of falling in love with incredible clarity in *All the Kings Men*. He wrote, "[W]hen you get in love you are made all over again. The person who loves you has picked you out of the great mass of uncreated clay which is humanity to make something out of, and the poor lumpish clay which is you wants to find out what it has been made into."[2]

That's the rush I wanted to feel. To be made new by the love of another. That was the great need, the loss I felt—therefore, the thing I most desired. To be chosen. To be recreated. To be seen as something loveable, something lovely, through the eyes of another. To be seen. To be known. To be loved. Forever. Unfortunately, fifteen-year-old girls and seventeen-year-old boys weren't built to give or hold that kind of love.

Loved to the End

In John 13, we encounter an awkward scene. Jesus has gathered His disciples into a rented room to share one last meal with His beloved friends before He faces His own death. He has some things to tell them, to teach them. He has more of Himself to share with them as they enjoy the Passover meal together. They enter the room to prepare for supper when they suddenly realize something is off. There are no slaves in the house to help make the proper preparations, the worst of which was washing all of their dirt-caked feet. I say the worst because that dirt wasn't nice Georgia red clay. It was full of all kinds of waste—animal, spoiled food, and human—per the reality of pre-modern world sanitary conditions.

This was certainly intentional on Jesus's part because it was a profound moment for Him to do two things: to show them the extent of His love for them and to teach them how to love one another. To show them that love is far more than romance or mere sentimentality. That true love looks like laying down your life for the good of others. Vulnerability is the posture of love, and Jesus is giving them an indelible image of what vulnerability looks like as He takes the form of a servant who kneels to wash their unclean feet.

That was the awkwardness that followed, that kind that made Peter object. But the first awkwardness was the posturing the disciples were doing up until that moment. John implies that none of the disciples signed up for the lowly task. The disciples of the well-known Jesus don't do that kind of thing. That belongs to hired hands, the people who *do* do that kind of thing. They weren't interested in the kind of love that takes the posture of a servant, as much as they were posturing themselves for positions of power when Jesus came into His kingdom. Peter objects because Jesus should know better than to lower himself to a task so beneath Him.

It needs to be said that the disciples weren't dumb. Sometimes preachers like me can give the impression that these men were always missing the point because they were slow of learning or hard of hearing. The reality is much worse. It wasn't that they were dumb; it was that they were learned in the ways of the world. They knew how power worked. They knew that those who have more of it can do more with it. It wasn't that they had somehow missed all of Jesus's teaching about His sacrificial death. It was that it didn't compute with the systems of power, religious or not, to which they were so accustomed. Thus, too, their confusion when a powerful rabbi coming into His kingdom picked up the towel and the basin and knelt at their feet. They were disarmed by the vulnerability of Jesus's love because true love is always disarming in that way. It lays down power for the sake of love as if to say you are more than what you've done and what you do.

This is what Jesus is doing before He saves the world. He isn't thinking about Himself, about the betrayal that will come from the man whose feet He is about to wash, about the injustice He will face or the painful death He is about to undergo. He is thinking about how to love His friends well. He *is* loving them well, taking their feet in His hands, washing them with warm water, wiping them with the towel wrapped about His waist. They have been thirsty for power. Jesus is giving them the love they don't yet know how much they need. The self-giving love of Jesus that washes away their sins even as He washes the dirt from their feet.

There's a scene in the documentary on Fred Rogers (better known as Mr. Rogers from *Mr. Rogers' Neighborhood*), *Won't You Be My Neighbor*, where they recount a powerful scene from the show. Mr. Rogers had noticed how racism was affecting public swimming pools around the country as white families refused to share pools with black families, racistly believing that somehow black children would spoil the water. So Mr. Rogers arranged a scene where he and a recurring African American character on the show would come home after work and soothe their feet together in a kid-sized swimming pool. It was, and still is, a powerful image. White feet sharing the same cleansing, cooling water with black feet. It was an image that put weight behind the theme of Fred Rogers's life, to convey to everyone that "they are loved, and capable of loving."

Fred Rogers was simply following the example of Jesus. It's why Jesus told Peter, "Unless you let Me wash your feet, you have no part with Me." He has come not to be served but to serve and to give His life as a ransom for all who know how their feet have rushed into sin. He has come to cleanse us from all the shameful places our need to be loved has driven us.

As Jesus kneels at their selfish, quarrelsome, power-hungry feet, He isn't disillusioned about them. He doesn't kneel to wash the feet of those who have lived clean lives. John says, "having loved His own in the world, He loved them to the end." He did not love them because they were so lovely, so influential, so powerful. Jesus didn't choose twelve influencers to change the world. He chose twelve flawed men to love. And He loved them to the very end of his life. He loved them to the very end of their lives. He is loving them to the very end of the world. He will love them eternally in the new Heaven and the new Earth. He loved them, loves them, and will love them with every ounce of love He has to give, and the good news is that love is infinite and it's the same love He has for you and for me. Because we are so well loved by Jesus, we indeed are capable of loving.

Loved to the End of Themselves

We recently closed on a house, and as we went to the closing, something strange happened. Because we were excited and hadn't closed on a house in a long time, my wife and I decided it would probably be appropriate to dress up a little. Not black tie formal, but slightly-ironic-date-night-at-Chili's formal. After all, I'm a pastor, and she's a stay-at-home mom, so our occasions to fancy it up a little are pretty slim. We show up, decked out in our Chili's finest, and there is the seller in gym clothes and flip flops. Now, maybe he had just come from working out, which is good for him, but the impression we had was that it was a total power move. It was if he was saying, "Oh, this means something to you? Cool. This is just a very chill day in my life."

As one who could make any power move look like an awkward side hug, part of me really respected it. But then it got me thinking about how naturally we fall into similar power moves as followers of Jesus, whose entire life was an anti-power move. I don't mean that we show up to closings in gym clothes and flip flops. I mean the way we crave and prefer power to the hard, mundane, often-unnoticed reality of love.

More and more studies are coming out that show how like the disciples we are when it comes to our love for power, admiration, and success. The studies I'm thinking of are about how many pastors are (or become?) narcissists. I'm no stranger myself to how easy it is for me to "do" ministry more in the name of being loved like Jesus than in the name of loving like Jesus. Yes, the Lord looks on the heart, but how are the rest of us supposed to tell the difference between a pastor who longs for their people to love Jesus and a pastor who longs for everyone to think he's a success?

Jean Vanier, the founder and leader of L'Arche, a community for the disabled, wrote about the temptation of power in the lives of all Christians:

"The need for power, acclaim and honours can undermine the message of Jesus and lead to a road of compromise with the values of society. We all imagine that if we had more money, more influence, and more power, we would be able to set things right. I am very familiar with this need to compromise, for it is something I sense in myself as well as my own communities. It is sometimes easier for me to accept the experience of being acclaimed for a book I have written or a talk I have given than just to sit down, poorly and humbly, and share my life lovingly with my brothers and sisters ... We all have to avoid getting caught up in the power game."[3]

I think about the scene in *Avengers: Infinity War* (spoiler alert) where Thanos faces the decision to save the life of his daughter Gamora and give up the infinity stone he covets or to sacrifice his daughter to gain it. He chooses to sacrifice her so that he can gain the power he needs to accomplish what he has set out to do. His choice is the choice set before all of us. We are always either sacrificing love for power or power for love.

Jesus is challenging His disciples in the upper room to choose to follow Him and sacrifice power for love. He is setting them an example of what it looks like. To kneel with those in need and humbly give yourself. To use all the authority, privilege, and position you've been given in this life and to use it for the cause and sake of love.

But it's more than an example He's setting. He's enacting on them His anointed work in their lives. To love them to the end of themselves. This is the real cleansing they so desperately need, the cleansing of sin, the cleansing of the love of the world and its ways. We so often think about love for the world as if it were merely a love for worldly goods or possessions or worldly pleasures, but we barely mention the more ingrained ways we smuggle worldly values into the church. Show me the church that prefers a pastor who preaches faithfully OK sermons but kneels to wash the feet of his people every day to the pastor who knocks it out of the park on Sundays, on top of having incredible vision for his business—ahem—church, yet doesn't have time to kneel with their people. We always either sacrifice love for power or power for love.

This is what Jesus is loving His disciples out of. How he's loving them to the end of themselves. He is loving them to the end of their love of power. He is loving them into the power of the love that gives itself freely—not for power, not for admiration, not for success—but so that our life together in Jesus would increase. It's the kind of love by which Jesus said the world would know that we are His.

One of my pastor friends loves to tell the story of a college Bible study. He had shown up early to the students' apartment to make sure things were ready and had stepped through the sliding glass door on the patio. As he was waiting, killing time, he started to take in his reflection on the tinted sliding glass door, doing the kind of things that we all do safely in the privacy of the mirrors in our own homes. Fixing his hair, smoothing out his clothes, admiring the progress he'd been making in the gym, when all of a sudden, he hears laugher coming from inside the apartment. He opens the sliding door where he's horrified to find his students have been watching him the whole time. He shares that story not because he's proud of it but because it was a humbling moment that helped him come more to the end of himself. Was he there to love these students or to love himself?

Are we here to love one another, to love our neighbors, the ones who already love Jesus and the ones who don't, or are we here to love ourselves? Dietrich Bonhoeffer said, "When Christ calls a man he bids him come and die." The work of Jesus in our lives is to love us out of our sins, away from our idols, to love us to the end of our own delusions of self-importance, the end of our power moves, that we might better know and share the love He has for us.

Loved to the End of Himself

The image Jesus gives His disciples, and us, is far better than a Hallmark card declaring His love. His love is more than sentiment, more than words. As He knelt, I'm not sure what Jesus was feeling at that moment. Did He feel love for them, or did He simply love them? The older I get, the more convinced I am that love is much less a feeling than it is a self-giving for another's sake.

I think about my mom after my dad left. She had no college degree, so finding a job to support two kids wasn't an option until she went back to school. So she did. She ground out a degree while she took care of the house, prepared meals for us, tucked us in at night, then got back to it. She showed me in those difficult years that love is a grind far more than a feeling. You grind for what you love, and thankfully, my mom loved us. She sacrificially gave herself for us that we might have a life.

After Jesus knelt to wash His disciples' feet, He sat with them to have supper. It was a typical Passover meal, except for one detail. Matthew records that there was bread and there was wine, but where was the lamb? There wasn't a lamb because the Lamb was seated at the table with them. The One who washed their feet with His hands is the Lamb who would wash away their sins with His blood.

In just days, we find Jesus kneeling again. But this time, He is agonizing in prayer. He knows where the Father is leading Him, but He anxiously cries out at the judgment He will undergo. *Isn't there another way? But not My will, but Yours be done*. We always either sacrifice love for power, or power for love. The good news for power-hungry people is that Jesus chose to sacrifice power for love.

It's good news for the love-hungry, too. The love we have been looking for isn't out there in another person somewhere. Or another job. Or another place. The Love we have been looking for is found in the One who holds all power and authority, with the Name above all names—and yet is right before us, the King of Love, kneeling at our feet.

CHAPTER 10

The Gardener

*"'Woman why are you weeping? Whom are you seeking?'
Supposing him to be the gardener, she said to him, 'Sir, if you have
carried him away, tell me where you have laid him, and I will take
him away.' Jesus said to her, 'Mary.' She turned and said to him
in Aramaic, 'Rabboni!'"*

John 20:15–16 (ESV)

*"What they were looking at was the first day of a new creation,
with a new heaven and a new earth; and in a semblance o
f the gardener God walked again in the garden, in the cool
not of the evening but of the dawn."*

GK Chesterton[1]

I come from a long line of gardeners. My mom has a green thumb, as they say, and has transformed every part of the yard around her house into lush green spaces. I suppose she learned it from my grandmother, who kept rows upon rows of bright roses, hydrangeas the size of cotton candy, and fickle azaleas she knew exactly how to tame. I can still picture my grandmother huddled around her roses, caring for them, grooming them, a mother of roses. I can also remember being the only grandchild she ever spanked after she had repeatedly told me not to pick the roses, and like Adam in the garden, I needed to see what would happen.

I come from a long line of gardeners, but I myself do not have a green thumb. Or maybe I do and am too lazy to test my potential gardening superpowers. My only real experience working with any kind of plant was a summer's worth of landscaping. It was enough to steer me away from making a living working with my hands. But I do remember the satisfying feeling of carving out a flower bed and fitting together pieces of sod as if it were a living puzzle. The satisfaction of plunging clean hands into dirt and making something, bringing life to a space that looks like death. Our biggest job that summer was laying sod and planting trees in the parking-lot islands of a new Walmart. Years later, I still love to drive through it when I'm in town and to tell my kids, "I did that."

John Stott once wrote about God that "he is both white collar and blue collar in his work. He knows how to organize and arrange, but he also isn't afraid to get his hands dirty." He plunged his hands into the dirt and brought new life, a man made in His image. It wasn't good that that he was alone, so He made a woman too, and then He set them to tend to a luscious garden, teeming with all kinds of life, all kinds of potential. We come from a long line of gardeners.

That's why I don't think it's a meaningless detail when John tells us that when the Risen Jesus, the Second Adam, first appeared to Mary, she mistook him for the gardener. She thought to herself, "Maybe this man who is here to tend the shrubs and flowers and grass around the tomb of Jesus knows something about where He is." She hasn't yet realized that the Risen Jesus is a Gardener of a different kind. He has come to recreate, to bring new life to fallen image bearers. He has turned the long sinful winter of the Fall to the new spring of resurrection hope. He has come to tend not to the shrubs and flowers and grass but to something else. The Risen Jesus has come to tend the tears and fears and doubts of His people.

Tending Our Tears

The first question the Risen Jesus asks Mary is "Why are you weeping?" You can almost hear the tenderness in His voice as He asks. It isn't a rebuke of her tears. He isn't scolding her, as if to say "Wake up dummy, it's Me." Sometimes it's easy for me to think of Jesus more like Tom Hanks in *A League of Their Own* in that classic scene where he gruffly barks at a sobbing Geena Davis, "There's no crying in baseball!"

There is crying in life with Jesus. One of the first things that drew me to Jesus was that I felt He might know what to do with my tears. I had grown up my whole life in the South and learned fairly quickly that neither men nor boys are supposed to show that kind of weakness. Walker Percy has pointed out that Christianity in the South has been much more influenced by the stoicism that values evenness, strength, putting on a brave face, and getting on with things than the emotional life we find in the Psalms and in the life of Jesus Himself. But as a twelve-year-old boy who had in one year experienced the loss of a father to drug addiction, the loss of a grandfather to a freak accident, and the loss of a friend to suicide, I needed a Savior who could teach me how to cry.

I needed to know how to cry. It's hard to pinpoint the exact moment when we "came of age," the moment where it's clear that the innocence of youth has faded and something much more brutal has replaced it. The moment when we know that life as we knew it has packed its bags and in through the front door is life from now on. Dan Allender likes to ask the question as he's helping men and women process their stories, "What are the moments in your life where you said out loud or to yourself, 'Life can never be the same'?" The year 1992 was that in spades for me. First dad, then my first two funerals. The first, my grandfather, who slipped on the concrete steps outside his house on the way to work, cracked his head, and fell into a coma from which he never woke.

The second, one of my friends and classmates who, after school one day, turned a shotgun to himself and bid farewell to the world. We were told it was an accident, and maybe it was. Or maybe he had come to the same stark realization about life that I had.

His funeral was the hardest. To watch the faces of seventh-grade boys turn from their typical teasing grins to grimaces stained and shrouded in tears is a fearful sight to behold. I watched my friends taking in death, trying to take in death myself, but does anyone know how to take it in? The adults around us weren't of much help because they were taking it in themselves, thinking of their own children, their own moments of life where they quietly said to themselves "Life can never be the same."

"Why are you weeping?" Jesus asks Mary, but He knows. She is weeping at the unfairness of life. She is weeping because her friend is dead. She is weeping because someone has stolen the body of the Rabbi she loved with all her heart. She is weeping because how is life supposed to go on when what has been your life is suddenly robbed from you? Taken like a purse off the street?

Then Jesus says her name. "Mary." You can almost hear the reassurance in His voice. He knows her tears, knows what to do with them. Her tears, as they cut small streams down her face, now begin to gather into the ocean that is Jesus's love for her. He sees her tears. Knows every moment in her life where she has whispered in the darkness, "Life can never be the same." And it's true. Life will never be the same. The Risen Jesus wipes away her tears by saying her name in such a way as to say, "Mary. I know. I know."

He does know. He is no stranger to tears. He has just cried a sea's worth in the Garden of Gethsemane, pleading that life would not be the way that it is. Pleading that the Father would take the cup of suffering from his plate. He knows our tears because He has His own. Because Jesus knows how to cry, He can teach us how to as well. Because Jesus has cried with us and for us, He is a safe place for our tears.

In Nicholas Wolterstorff's memoir on losing his son to a freak mountain climbing accident, *Lament for a Son*, he shares some beautiful and poignant thoughts about tears. He writes, "I've thought a lot about tears. Our culture says we must be strong and that strength in sorrow is to be seen in a tearless face. Tears are signs of weakness ... But why celebrate tearlessness? Why insist on never outwarding the inward when that inward is bleeding? Does enduring while crying not require as much strength as never crying? Must we always mask our suffering? May we not sometimes allow people to see and enter it? Why is it so important to act "strong" in this way? ... No, I shall not pretend. Instead, I shall look at the world through tears. And in doing so, perhaps ... I shall see things that dry-eyed I could not see ... [one of] those who have caught a glimpse of God's new day, who ache with all their being for that day's coming, and who break out into tears when confronted with its absence."[2]

He calls those teary-eyed mourners "aching visionaries," those who see the world through tears, and entrust those tears to the Risen Jesus. I was first drawn to Jesus because I thought maybe He could handle my tears, and He has shown me, through His own tears, that He knows exactly what to do with them.

Tending Our Fears

The Risen Jesus first appears to Mary, and the next place He shows up is in the midst of a room full of terrified disciples. They are mourning in their own ways, trying to figure out what to with their lives from here. And they are afraid. Terrified that somehow they too will die like Jesus, nearly sure that the Jews who tried Jesus will come for them next. As Jesus enters that room, their fear is palpable, sucking all the oxygen into a vortex of anxiety. How will The Gardener tend to their fears?

I'll admit that, though I've wrestled with depression for most of my life, anxiety is less familiar to me. I don't know its frenzied liturgy, haven't felt its paralyzing power. But I am learning, as the husband of sixteen years to an anxious wife. My first real moment trying to tend to my wife's anxiety was an utter disaster. She had recently lost her father to multiple myeloma and was struggling with everything it means to lose a parent long before you think you'll ever lose one. One night, we were watching *Breaking Bad* in bed when suddenly a combination of swelling in her throat and the general anxiety a show like *Breaking Bad* can induce came together in a perfect storm where she slipped into a full-blown panic attack. Let's just say the way I handled it would have been worthy of a divorce. She asked me to call an ambulance, to which I said, "You're just having a panic attack," breaking Rule Number One of how to help someone having a panic attack. Oddly, pointing that fact out to them doesn't help. So she called an ambulance herself, in true Proverbs 31 woman fashion, to which I then said, "Do you know how much this is going to cost?" which again, oddly did not help the situation. (Remember, I said this was probably divorce-worthy behavior.) When the medics showed up, they were able to ease the panic attack, but unfortunately, there wasn't a team of marriage therapists behind them to help ease everything else.

Of course, there is a crucial difference between a panic attack and simply being afraid. I don't mean at all to say that Jesus tending to our anxiety precludes the help of doctors, counselors, and medicine. If you've ever had or witnessed a panic attack, you immediately say a prayer of thanksgiving for God's gift of medicine. There's a way of over-spiritualizing anxiety as if the fall never touched our brains and bodies that in the end is far less spiritual than it seems.

Whatever the clinical anxiety of the disciples (looking at you, Peter), Jesus is speaking to their fear on account of what has happened in their lives. They are afraid of what will happen to them. They are afraid that they will be scattered and end up alone. They are afraid of what the authorities will do to them. They are afraid because they trusted Jesus and it didn't work out. They are afraid of how they'll make a living. They are afraid of what life looks like after you know it can never be the same.

And Jesus's first words to them are, "Peace be with you." It feels, at first, like the Nazarene version of "it will all work out" that I can hear thousands of Southern moms say to their now-adult children, who can almost hear them closing their little copies of *Jesus Calling* having just read the devotional for today. And those adult children want to scream into a pillow because it seemed like a nice way of saying "You should just trust the Lord" without ever asking what might be causing the particular flavor of panic of the day. At first, this greeting from Jesus seems dismissive. Like Jesus is rebuking them in a passive-aggressive way. But Jesus is never passive-aggressive, and for that, I am thankful because it means He is not like me.

"Peace be with you." Part of what Jesus is saying is something the Risen Jesus alone can say. He is saying that the things we should really be afraid of, the sin that separates, the death that threatens, the spiritual forces of evil that roam, they cannot touch us like they once did. Not that we won't sin, won't die, won't fall prey to Satan's schemes. We will. But that by His resurrection we now have peace with God; therefore, not even the gates of Hell can prevail against those who are securely in the arms of the Risen Jesus. The things we should truly be afraid of, Jesus has conquered in such a way that the war is over. The Prince of Peace has accomplished a peace on our behalf that we could never have accomplished ourselves. We are safe in His care.

But He is also saying, "Peace be with you" because Peace is with them. Jesus, who is our peace, is with them, in that room, that very moment. Their fears are swirling, circling them, ready to devour. But Peace is with them. A Peace that protects. A Peace that guards. Jesus isn't asking them not to be afraid. Jesus is asking them to bring their fears to Him. Karl Barth once wrote that "courage is fear that has said its prayers." Jesus not only knows what to do with our tears, He knows what to do with our fears as well. He walks through the locked door of that room, through the locked doors of their hearts, and says, "Trust Me with your fears."

Jean Vanier puts it beautifully. He writes, "When we are frightened, don't we, too, hide behind the locked doors of our hearts, unable to reach out towards others? Yet, Jesus comes to each of us through these locked doors and says: 'Peace to you!' At a level that is deeper than all that is wounded and fearful in us, Jesus reveals that He loves us and forgives us for all our inconstancies. We are unique and precious to Him. We are the beloved children of God. Jesus will always be with us in all the pain and joy we will live in the journey of life."[3]

Tending Our Doubts

There is one disciple missing in the room that night. Thomas. We know him best as Doubting Thomas, but something like Honest Thomas or Skeptical Thomas or Enneagram Five Thomas is probably fairer. It's easy for us who know the rest of the story to minimize the confusion and pain these men and women were feeling. The Lord they had left everything to follow was dead. Their dreams were dashed, a broken glass shattered on the kitchen floor of their lives. While the rest of the disciples were huddled in fear, Thomas had left to figure things out for himself. That takes some courage. Thomas had taken a walk that day. Sometimes the most spiritual thing you can do is go for a long walk.

When he gets back, the disciples tell him about seeing Jesus, back from the dead. Dead people don't live again, so Thomas probably chalks it up to an excited, though misguided, delusion that anxious people often come up with. He loves his friends, but come on. How could Jesus possibly be alive? Dead people don't live again.

So Jesus shows up again, and this time, Thomas is there. He has heard what Thomas said—that he would never believe until he touched the wounds of Jesus, in the flesh. Jesus walks right over to Thomas, gently, the way you approach a scared animal, and says, "Put your finger here, and see My hands." Maybe this scene is what Peter had in mind when he wrote, "By His wounds you have been healed." By touching the wounds of Jesus, Thomas's doubts were healed.

Doubts, when they are genuine, aren't an obstacle to faith in Jesus. They are an invitation. An invitation to taste and see that the Lord is good, and part of His goodness to us is welcoming our doubts. There are doubts that, if you look beneath the surface, aren't really doubts at all. Instead, they are attempts at autonomy masquerading as doubts, a way of asking questions when you already know the answer, or so you believe.

Then there are doubts that are more honest, more humble. They aren't declarations of autonomy but invitations to have your mind changed. You can almost picture Thomas setting up a booth similar to the popular meme, one that says, "Jesus is dead. Change my mind." The Risen Jesus slowly approached his little booth, and his mind was forever changed. So much so that he is the first worshipper of the Risen Jesus, as he exults, "My Lord and My God!"

Doubts aren't a threat to the Risen Jesus; neither should we treat them as such. Some of the best questions come from those who aren't yet sure what to do with Jesus. Often, it's too risky for those already safely inside the fold of Christian community to be honest about their doubts. When you know what you are supposed to believe, how can you be honest about the struggle you're having to believe what you're supposed to believe? But Jesus makes space for Thomas. Gives him time. He doesn't condemn him for not believing the Good News at first. Instead, he meets Thomas in his questions. He knows what to do with Thomas's doubts. He knows what to do with ours too.

In a culture that is quick to speak and slow to listen, followers of Jesus have a chance to be radically, refreshingly countercultural simply by listening more. Eugene Peterson once wrote, "We often ask how many people have you spoken to about Christ this week. But I like to ask, how many people have you listened to in Christ this week?" It's in the listening that our stories are shared. A culture that does not listen to one another quickly becomes a culture that is fragmented, polarized. We fail to love each other because we fail to listen. And we fail to listen to each other because we fail to love.

Jesus does neither with Thomas. Or, rather, He does both. Because He loves Thomas, He listens to his doubts. And by listening to his doubts, He knows precisely how to love him. *Place your finger here. See My hands. Believe. Don't disbelieve.* It's not a rebuke. It's an invitation. In our doubts, our wounds are often open for all to see. The wounds of life in a fallen world. The dead don't live again, yet Thomas touched One who did. He touched the wounds of the One who died that we might live and lives that we may never truly die. And by His wounds, we are healed.

Edward Shillito, a Free Church minister in England during the First World War, once penned a poem about the healing wounds of Jesus, no doubt in response to the trauma the young men who saw and heard and did things at war they would spend a lifetime trying to forget. Shillito wrote,

Our wounds are hurting us; where is the balm?
Lord Jesus, by Thy Scars, we claim Thy grace.
If, when the doors are shut, Thou drawest near,
Only reveal those hands, that side of Thine;
We know to-day what wounds are, have no fear,
Show us Thy Scars, we know the countersign.
The other gods were strong; but Thou wast weak;
They rode, but Thou didst stumble to a throne;
But to our wounds only God's wounds can speak,
And not a god has wounds, but Thou alone.[4]

Show us Thy Scars. We, like Thomas, know the countersign.

CHAPTER 11

Breakfast with Jesus

*"As I read the Gospel of John again and again, I believe that
he is telling us about the presence of Jesus in our ordinary lives ...
Jesus meets us wherever we are. We do not have to do extraordinary
things, but to love and serve others in the name of the risen Jesus.
It all sounds so simple, though in reality it is not. In our everyday lives,
conflicts arise so easily. Relationships can be difficult. How do I work
with others? How do I nourish friendships? How do I accept the
unexpected and the accidents of life?"*

Jean Vanier[1]

"Jesus said to them, 'Come and have breakfast.'"
John 21:12 (NIV)

I fell in love with everything that breakfast can be at a Waffle House. I had already loved breakfast, have always loved breakfast. Breakfast is my ride or die. I was the kid that would eat a whole pan of Pillsbury Orange Danish Rolls, then a couple more bowls of Cinnamon Toast Crunch after. I was the kid who would walk into my grandmother's house at three o'clock in the afternoon and say, "Mimi, I want something that starts with a B," and she would graciously make me a pan of her legendary biscuits from scratch, as if I were some kind of breakfast tyrant.

Now that I'm older, I've tried my own hand at breakfast. I've discovered the magical world of mimosas and Bloody Marys. I've splurged on high-end cured bacon, like Benton's. I've almost perfected a cathead biscuit recipe for the cast iron pan I invested in a few years back. That cast iron pan is like my fifth child, and it might be my favorite. I've learned how to save bacon grease to up my egg game and my grits game. Did I mention that I really love breakfast?

Waffle House, though, made me fall even more in love. The perfection that is their hash browns. Their aggressively average coffee that makes everyone feel welcomed. Why wouldn't you want a T-bone steak with those eggs? Not feeling a steak? How about a patty melt so flawlessly greasy it fell from Heaven? Or maybe the cooks are angels in our midst? Waffle House taught me that breakfast is for all times and all people, that breakfast has healing powers—the power to bring unlikely characters together.

No one has captured the beauty of Waffle House better than Anthony Bourdain, shortly after his friend Sean Brock took him there for the first time. He wrote, "It is indeed marvelous—an irony-free zone where everything is beautiful and nothing hurts; where everybody regardless of race, creed, color, or degree of inebriation is welcomed."[2]

I'm not sure how Jesus will welcome us to the new Heaven and new Earth, but I hope He leads us all to an enormous Waffle House to feast with Him. Whether that happens or not, that is something close to what he does with Peter and a few other disciples by the Sea of Tiberias in John 21. They, in shame, have gone back to their jobs as local fishermen, but Jesus, in joy, has come to cook breakfast for them.

A Familiar Place

It's no mistake that this meal takes place by the Sea of Tiberius. It's the place some of the disciples had gone back to because it is the place where, before leaving to follow Jesus, they lived and made a living. It's where Jesus met them for the first time, calling them to come and follow Him. And it's the place where Jesus meets them for the second time, to call them back to Himself. It's reminiscent of Jonah 3, "the word of the Lord came to Jonah a second time." That's how the grace of God in Christ is. He comes the first time, the second time, the third time, as many times as it takes to bring us in repentance back to Himself. God's grace is more stubborn than our sin.

The presence of the Lord is everywhere. We know there is nowhere we can flee His Spirit. Yet there are places where the Lord first met us that will forever remain sweet to us. The Lord first met me at two local churches in my hometown—one the Episcopal church my family attended, and the other a Methodist church with a youth group my friends loved and invited me to join. Both of these places impacted me as a young Christian. They are where I learned to pray, to study Scripture, to sing my heart out to the Lord, to confess sin, to share life together in community. There were men and women there in that season for whom I am eternally grateful as they invited me into their homes, led small-group Bible studies, shared books that changed me—in short, they loved me like Jesus loved them.

So it was not lost on me when, after a hard season of wandering in college, full mostly of depression but also an unfortunate streak of drowning in sexual sin, that the Lord brought me back to both places. First, to work as intern at my hometown Episcopal church, then to serve as an interim youth minister at the Methodist church. I had barely graduated college when I went back home with my tail between my legs, trying to figure out what in the world to do with my life, depressed as ever. But the word of the Lord came a second time. He took me back to the very places I first met

Him, and there He renewed me, restored me to life with Him. He is, after all, the Good Shepherd who goes seeking lost sheep that He might bring them back home with great joy.

Frederick Buechner wrote about that feeling of lostness we've all felt in our lives, whether before or even after Christ. He writes, "For Adam and Eve, time started with their expulsion from the garden ... For all the sons and daughters of Eve, it starts at whatever moment it is at which the unthinking and timeless innocence of childhood ends, which may be either a dramatic moment ... or a moment or series of moments so subtle and undramatic that we scarcely recognize them. But one way or another the journey through time starts for us all, and for all of us, too, that journey is in at least one sense the same journey because what it is primarily, I think, is a journey *in search* ... We search for a self to be. We search for other selves to love. We search for work to do. And since even when to one degree or another we find these things, we find also that there is still something crucial missing which we have not found, we search for that unfound thing too, even though we do not know its name or where it is to be found or even if it is to be found at all."[3]

This is precisely the place the disciples find themselves in, searching for what has been lost. It's the place I found myself in right after college. It's a place all of us are familiar with, the place where we feel so lost and are desperately trying to find what we have lost. Or what we need to make us whole again.

This is the place Jesus invites them to have breakfast with Him. This is the place where Jesus shows up. The very places where we feel most lost are the very places He finds us, to remind us that He has come to seek and save those who have lost their way, lost themselves. He is a seeker in that way, a searcher. His eyes waiting to meet our eyes to tell us the way home. These disciples are searching for fish, but Jesus is searching for them. He has come to bring them home to Himself.

A Familiar Meal

At first, they don't recognize Jesus. This is the last place they expected Him to show up. At first, all they see and hear is a man shouting to them about their fishing. They don't immediately recognize His voice and must have been mildly annoyed that a random stranger on the beach would have the audacity to tell experienced fishermen like themselves where to lay their nets. There's nothing worse than a stranger telling you how to do your job.

They must have been desperate, though, because they listened. The next thing, they had caught more fish than they knew what to do with. This is the moment, this moment of sheer abundance, where Peter recognizes the Lord. Jesus had told them He had come to give them abundant life, and in this moment, it includes a generous amount of fish for Jesus to make a breakfast feast for His tired and hungry friends.

Jean Vanier writes, "Everything seems so ordinary, even this miracle. They just put the net on the other side of the boat and were lucky! This is not the same as the extraordinary event at Cana or the multiplication of bread and fish. Those events were seen by everybody. Here, Jesus is on the shore and has prepared breakfast for these hungry, tired men. All is so simple, so loving. Jesus cares so much for them."[4]

Ordinariness is not something I've ever been comfortable with. Life is supposed to happen in big moments, not small ones. Grandiosity can be a struggle for me. I want to feel great feelings, eat great meals, drink great drinks, watch great movies, read great books, go on great trips, have a great time. I have a hard time, in the words of Updike, "to give the mundane its beautiful due."[5] My wife likes to joke that I need a standing ovation for taking out the garbage. To me, life is supposed to happen in big moments, not small ones.

This moment between Jesus and these six disciples is a small one. It is a simple miracle. A simple meal. Yet what Jesus is doing is so huge. Conversation over a meal is how Jesus loves these men back to Himself, back to themselves. Simple hospitality, in the hands of Jesus, can bring great healing. Jesus is giving the mundane its beautiful due because often that is the most spiritual thing on earth to do.

The beautiful thing about Jesus is that He meets us in the ordinariness of life. He meets us where we are, not where we should be. He meets us in the loneliness of our Friday nights as we polish off another season on Netflix. He meets us in the lingering marital fights that push past the weekend into Monday, Tuesday morning. He meets us in the awkwardness that is our families and the difficulty that can be our children. He meets us, too, in the very places we most hate ourselves and wish we could be anyone else. Jesus pursues us, reaches out for us, not in the extraordinary moments of life, but the most ordinary ones, like a simple breakfast with tired, hungry friends on the beach.

One of my favorite Robin Williams roles is a lesser-known one in a movie called *The Fisher King*. The story is about a proud, ambitious radio host (think Howard Stern), played by Jeff Bridges, who, because of some careless words he speaks one night, causes a listener to go on a shooting spree. Williams plays the husband of a woman killed by the shooter that night. After losing his wife, he goes insane and ends up on the streets. Soon after, Bridges's character loses his job and finds himself out drinking on the street a lot, too. This is where the two meet and become a source of healing in each other's lives.

The scene in the movie (from which it gets its title) is when Williams tells Bridges a strange story about The Fisher King, which has become the obsession of his life. He says,

"Did you ever hear the story of the Fisher King? It begins with the king as a boy having to spend the night alone in a forest so he could become the king. And while he's spending the night alone, he's visited by a sacred vision. Out of the fire appears The Holy Grail, a symbol of God's divine grace. And a voice said to the boy, 'You shall be keeper of the grail so that it may heal the hearts of men.' But the boy was blinded by greater visions of a life filled with power, glory, and beauty. And in his state of radical amazement, he felt for a brief moment, not like a boy, but invincible, a god. So he reached into the fire to take the Grail ... and the Grail vanished, leaving him with his hand in the fire to be terribly wounded.

"Now as this boy grew older, his wound grew deeper—until, one day, life for him lost its reason. He had no faith in any man, not even himself. He couldn't love—or feel loved. He was sick with experience. He began to die. One day, a fool wandered into the castle and found the king alone. Now, being a fool, he was simple-minded. He didn't see a king. He only saw a man alone and in pain. And he asked the king, 'What ails you, friend?' The king replied, 'I'm thirsty and I need some water to cool my throat.' So the fool took a cup from beside his bed and filled it with water and handed it to the king. And as the king began to drink, he realized that his wound was healed. He looked at his hands and there—there was the Holy Grail, that which he had sought his whole life. He turned to the fool and said with amazement, 'How could you find that which my brightest and bravest could not?' The fool replied, 'I don't know. I only knew that you were thirsty.' "[6]

It is in the ordinariness of life, the cooking of breakfast, the getting a thirsty man a cup of water, that the grace of God is most often found.

How much grace have we missed in our thirst to be extraordinary?

A Familiar Fire

When the disciples made their way up the shore to Jesus, they found Him cooking on a charcoal fire. Part of how you know you can trust Jesus is He cooked with charcoal. Smoked meat (even fish) covers a multitude of sins. This charcoal fire, though, was no accident. Jesus is doing something very pointed in the life of Peter, who, of all the disciples, may have been carrying the most shame.

Just weeks before, it was around a similar charcoal fire that he had denied even knowing Jesus. Jesus had warned him that he would do the thing he swore he would never do. Often, that's what it takes to learn grace: Jesus allowing us to fall into sin we swore we never would. Not that we would live in shame for the rest of our lives but that we might learn something about the kind of sinners we really are and the kind of grace we really need.

Shortly after I became a Christian, there was a purity movement that swept youth groups nationwide. It felt to me like Promise Keepers, but for teenagers and lasered in on sex specifically. Books like Joshua Harris's *I Kissed Dating Goodbye* and things like purity rings and future wife/husband journals were flying off the shelves of LifeWays. I never had a purity ring, but I was wholeheartedly behind the movement. It's like Jesus said, "The world will know you are My disciples because you are virgins."

I was determined to save myself for marriage. Never mind the porn problem I had been nursing since middle school that would soon devour me whole. No pre-marital sex for this guy!

It's funny how great that sounds when you're not in an actual relationship. Soon after my pledged devotion to purity, I got a girlfriend. Everything started innocently enough. I staged our first kiss during the "Kiss the Girl" scene in *The Little Mermaid*, like the youth group weirdo I was. What I underestimated, though, was how lust works. You tell yourself there are lines you will never cross, and lust winks back at you and says, "Sure" with a heavy dose of sarcasm. Because lust knows that if you just give it enough time and space, it will work itself through your relationship like yeast. I've never made bread (Christian fail), but I think that's how yeast works.

It's often the things we said we would never do that come back to haunt us. That was Peter. "Even though all these fall away, I will never fall away," he said with pride. "Even though everyone denies you, I will never deny you," he said, showing how little he really knew himself. Next thing he knows, he's around that charcoal fire, and a little girl makes the connection, and he's screaming, "I don't f-ing know him!" The other shoe has now dropped, and Peter can't get out of bed, which is now stained with tears of regret.

How does Jesus meet us in our failure? How does He meet us after we have done the very things we said we would never do? He meets us like He met Elijah on the verge of suicide, in a still small voice with food and sleep. He meets us like Isaiah told us He would meet us, with a gentleness that doesn't break bruised reeds or snuff out faintly burning wicks. He meets us like he met Peter on the beach, around a charcoal fire as if to say, "Of course, I know what you've done, and

172

of course, I will always love you. Now here. Eat some bread and fish."

There's a scene in *The Big Kahuna* I wish every Christian would watch. In it, Danny Devito plays a seasoned salesman, and Peter Facinelli plays a young, ambitious evangelical who is full of himself. In the scene, Phil (Devito) is rebuking Bob (Facinelli) for his pride and arrogance. Phil says, "We were talking before about character. You were asking me about character ... But the question is much deeper than that. The question is, do you have any character at all? And if you want my honest opinion, Bob, you do not. For the simple reason that you don't regret anything yet."

Bob responds, "Are you saying I won't have any character unless I do something I regret?"

Phil: "No, Bob. I'm saying you've already done plenty of things to regret, you just don't know what they are. It's when you discover them, when you see the folly in something you've done, and you wish that you had it to do over, but you know you can't, because it's too late. So you pick that thing up, and you carry it with you to remind you that life goes on, the world will spin without you, you really don't matter in the end. *Then* you will obtain character, because honesty will reach out from inside and tattoo itself all across your face. Until that day, however, you cannot expect to go beyond a certain point."

This is that moment for Peter. He has done plenty of things he should have regretted, but in his denial, he can no longer deny his regret. This is where Jesus meets him by the fire, heals his regret, undoes his shame, restores him to the love he has for Jesus, which is now more honest and therefore stronger. And now Peter is ready to build His church. Now Peter is ready to feed His sheep. Now Peter is ready to preach the Gospel Jesus has just preached to him by that charcoal fire.

It's not that we don't have plenty to regret. We do. It's when Jesus begins graciously revealing to us just how much we have to regret that the real work of healing begins. We are the people of many regrets. But He is the God of second, of third, of infinite chances. Not chances to prove ourselves. Chances to return again to Him, to confess what we regret, and to feel Him pick us up, to put us on our feet, that we might walk with Him again by the shore.

Conclusion

As I sit to write this morning, a contractor is looking at one of our kids' bathrooms upstairs. My wife and I felt confident this summer that we could remodel it ourselves. We (she, mostly) gutted the whole thing, ordered a new vanity and a new bathtub. That was July, and it's now November. We got stuck. We got overwhelmed. We needed help. Hence, the contractor came here this morning—and, hopefully, he won't quote us a year's worth of Ivy League college tuition to do the job.

This bathroom is just the starting place. Then there is the master bathroom. After that, a kitchen ceiling that is stained from water damage. After that, a kitchen floor that is peeling. I could go on. The point is that the work feels never-ending. There is an unlimited number of things we could do to make our house cozier, but there is not unlimited money. That's reality, and reality is not my favorite place to live.

The whole thing reminds me of one of my favorite C.S. Lewis quotes. He wrote,

"Imagine yourself as a living house. God comes in to rebuild that house. At first, perhaps, you can understand what He is doing. He is getting the drains right and stopping the leaks in the roof and so on; you knew that those jobs needed doing and so you are not surprised. But presently He starts knocking the house about in a way that hurts abominably and does not seem to make any sense. What on earth is He up to? The explanation is that He is building quite a different house from the one you thought of—throwing out a new wing here, putting on an extra floor there, running up towers, making courtyards. You thought you were being made into a decent little cottage: but He is building a palace. He intends to come and live in it Himself."[1]

I think this is why so many of us love HGTV. We get to watch a broken-down house be transformed into something we would love to live in ourselves. And whether we know it or not, it becomes a kind of metaphor for ourselves. Is it possible that someone could love us from a broken-down house into the kind of place that makes others feel at home? Is there a spiritual Chip and Joanna Gaines who can help this fixer-upper?

The problem, of course, with HGTV shows is that they make this kind of work seem relatively easy. They condense weeks', months', sometimes years' worth of work into a neat sixty-minute episode. Not so with the work of Jesus in our lives. Yes, He can make fixer-uppers beautiful again. And, yes, it will take a lifetime. There will be seasons where you wonder what He is doing. There will be times where you feel the work is taking far too long.

The key is to remember that He knows what He is doing. It was no accident that before He became the Savior of the world, He was an experienced carpenter. He knows how to build things, how to repair them. He loves to take broken things and make them whole again. It is His work. It is His way. He makes the broken beloved.

People like us most of all.

Endnotes

Introduction

[1] Charitie Lees Bancroft, "Before the Throne of God Above," 1863.

Chapter 1: A World of Brokenness

[1] Eugene Peterson, *The Message: The Bible in Contemporary Language* (Carol Stream: Nav-Press Publishing, 2002).

[2] Henri J. M. Nouwen, *Life of the Beloved: Spiritual Living in a Secular World* (New York: The Crossroad Publishing, 2002), 30.

[3] Raymond Carver, "Late Fragment," in *A New Path to the Waterfall* (New York: Atlantic Monthly Press, 1989).

[4] Tim Keller, "Preaching to the Heart," lectures delivered at Gordon Conwell Seminary's Pastor Builder series, 2006.

Chapter 2: The Wine Always Runs Out

[1] Jean Vanier, *Drawn into the Mystery of Jesus through the Gospel of John* (New York: Paulist Press, 2004), 59.

[2] Patterson Hood, "Daddy Needs a Drink," Razor and Tie Music, 2008.

[3] George Herbert, "The Agonie," 1633, from *Complete English Poems* (New York: Penguin Classics, 2005).

[4] N. T. Wright, "John 2.1–11, A Sermon at the Wedding of Michael Lloyd and Abigail Doggett in St Peter's Church, Ugley," n.d.

[5] Paul Miller, *Love Walked Among Us* (Carol Stream: NavPress, 2014).

[6] Waterdeep, "Both of Us'll Feel the Blast," written by Don Chaffer, *Sink or Swim*, 1997.

Chapter 3: Our Need for Grace

[1] Flannery O'Connor, *The Habit of Being: Letters of Flannery O'Connor* (New York: Farrar, Straus and Giroux, 1988).

[2] Jerry Bridges, *The Discipline of Grace: God's Role and Our Role in the Pursuit of Holiness,* (Carol Stream: NavPress, 2006).

[3] Michael Horton, *Christless Christianity* (Grand Rapids: Baker, 2008), 15.

[4] N.T Wright, *Simply Christian* (New York: HarperOne, 2010), 205.

[5] In the words of J. C. Ryle, "Would we know whether we are really converted? Would we know the test by which we must try ourselves? The surest mark of true conversion is humility." *Expository Thoughts on the Gospels: Matthew*, (Edinburgh: Banner of Truth, 1986), 220.

Chapter 4: Even Disciples Get Jealous Sometimes

[1] Henri Nouwen, ibid., 103.

[2] Donald Miller, *Blue Like Jazz: Nonreligious Thoughts on Christian Spirituality* (Nashville: Thomas Nelson, 2003).

[3] Fyodor Dostoevsky, "The Dream of a Ridiculous Man," in *The Best Stories of Fyodor Dostoevsky*, trans. David Magarshack (New York: Random House, 1992, 2001), 314.

[4] John Newton, "Letter IV to the Rev. Mr. R, April 18, 1776," in *The Works of the Rev. John Newton* (New York: Robert Carter Pub, 1844), 336.

Chapter 5: The Loneliness of Shame

[1] Jean Vanier, ibid., 96.

[2] The Avett Brothers, "Shame," lyrics by Robert Crawford, Scott Avett, Timothy Avett, BMG, 2007.

[3] William Cowper, *Letter to John Newton*, June 17, 1783.

[4] Ed Welch, "Depression's Odd Filter," CCEF blog, January 10, 2011.

[5] Malcolm Muggeridge, *Jesus, Rediscovered* (Carol Stream: Tyndale, 1973).

[6] C.S. Lewis, *The Silver Chair* (New York: HarperCollins, 2002 [1953]).

[7] Quoted in Kenneth Bailey, *Jesus Through Middle Eastern Eyes* (Westmont: IVP Academic, 2008).

Chapter 6: Do You Want to Be Whole?

[1] Jean Vanier, ibid., 104.

[2] Henri Nouwen, ibid., 94.

[3] Jonathan Franzen, *The Corrections* (New York: Picador, 2002), 263.

[4] C.S. Lewis, *The Voyage of the Dawn Treader*, (New York: HarperCollins, 2002 [1952]).

[5] Jean Vanier, ibid., 108.

[6] The National, "England," lyrics by Aaron Dessner, Matthew D. Berninger, BMG, 2010.

Chapter 7: Can't You See? Oh, Can't You See? What Those Pharisees Have Been Doing to Me

[1] Jean Vanier, ibid., 112, 114.

[2] Vintage 21 church, on *YouTube*, for their *Real Jesus* sermon series

[3] Flannery O'Connor, "The Turkey," in *The Complete Stories* (New York: Farrar, Straus and Giroux, 1971).

[4] Brennan Manning, *The Ragamuffin Gospel* (New York: Multnomah, 2005).

[5] CS. Lewis, *Letters to Malcom: Chiefly on Prayer* (New York: HarperOne, 2017 [1964]).

[6] Frederick Backman, *A Man Called Ove: A Novel* (New York: Washington Square Press, 2015).

Chapter 8: A Love Stronger Than Death

[1] Frederick Dale Bruner, *The Gospel of John: A Commentary* (Grand Rapids: Eerdmans, 2012).

[2] Henri Nouwen, *Letters to Marc About Jesus* (New York: HarperOne, 2009).

[3] Jean Vanier, ibid., 199.

[4] C.S. Lewis, *The Voyage of the Dawn Treader* (London: Geoffrey Bles, 1952).

[5] From his sermon "Truth, Tears, Anger, and Grace," preached in New York City at Redeemer Presbyterian Church, September 11, 2001.

Endnotes

Chapter 9: Loved to the End

[1] Frederick Buechner, *The Faces of Jesus: A Life Story* (Orleans: Paraclete Press, 2006).
[2] Robert Penn Warren, *All the King's Men* (New York: Harcourt Brace & Co., 1946).
[3] Jean Vanier, ibid., 238.

Chapter 10: The Gardener

[1] G. K. Chesterton, *The Everlasting Man, The Collected Works of G.K. Chesterton*, Volume 2 (San Francisco: Ignatius, 1986), 2: 344–345.
[2] Nicholas Wolterstorff, *Lament for a Son* (Grand Rapids: Eerdmans, 1987).
[3] Jean Vanier, ibid., 341.
[4] Edward Shillito, "Jesus of the Scars," 1919, n.p.

Chapter 11: Breakfast with Jesus

[1] Jean Vanier, ibid., 350.
[2] From Anthony Bourdain's TV show *Parts Unknown*, Season 8, Episode 6, "Charleston, SC," CNN.
[3] Frederick Buechner, *The Sacred Journey: A Memoir of Early Days* (New York: HarperOne, 1991).
[4] Jean Vanier, ibid., 349.
[5] John Updike, "Smoke Signals," *The Guardian*, January 9, 2004.
[6] *The Fisher King*, written by Richard LaGravenese, directed by Terry Gilliam, Tristar Pictures, 1991.

Conclusion

[1] C.S. Lewis, *Mere Christianity* (London: Geoffrey Bles, 1952).